May God's
Word always
be Real to
you too!

♡

Kimberly
Preston

Credits:

Author: *Kimberly Preston*

Book and Launch Strategy: *Toni Purry*

Graphic Design and Art Direction: *Joanna Holden, modularink.com*

Front and Back Cover Photography: *Bree McCool*

Content Editor: *Lydia Mack & Pastor John Steward*

Proofreaders: *Kim Houser & Kristen Benjamin*

Event and Location Visionary: *Cheri Griswold*

Ever-willing, insightful Male Perspective: *Garry Goodwin*

Cheerleader and Hopes n' Dreams Accountability Partner: *Toni Cornelison*

Thank You to the countless amount of *friends and family* who've allowed me to write about our shared experiences that give glory to God and to His Word.

Special Thanks to my sons, *Blake and Ryan* for supporting and inspiring me to want to share my story with all the world. Also to my *Terrific Mom*, who encouraged me daily to "go write" and then cried with me as I read each story back to her. You've always graciously shown me how to persevere despite obstacles. And above all, I thank *Our Lord God* who displays His love for me daily and is the strength in my many weaknesses.

To learn more about the organizations and inspirations mentioned in this book visit my website @kimberlypreston.com

*The NIV Study Bible is the source of all Scripture references.

1977

DEDICATED TO AL PRESTON

...for being the kind of dad that made
the idea of having a loving, Heavenly Father
an easy concept for me to understand.

TABLE OF CONTENTS

9	Introduction	
10	20/20 Vision	GENESIS
14	This Move Will Take a Miracle	EXODUS
21	Image Management	LEVITICUS
25	Journey to the Land of Promise	NUMBERS
29	The Gift of the Sabbath	DEUTERONOMY
34	The Walls Came Tumbling Down	JOSHUA
38	A Gal Like Gideon	JUDGES
44	Where you Go, I Go	RUTH
49	Letting Go	1 & 2 SAMUEL
54	Touching Eternity	1 & 2 KINGS
58	Back To Africa	1 & 2 CHRONICLE
63	Not Ours But His	EZRA
68	A New Perspective	NEHEMIAH
73	For Such a Time as This	ESTHER
76	He's Got a Chapter 42 for You	JOB
80	Fearfully and Wonderfully Made	PSALMS
85	Iron Sharpens Iron	PROVERBS
88	I'm Pro-Choice Too!	ECCLESIASTES
91	Lullaby	SONG OF SONGS
95	Clouds of Hope	ISAIAH
100	Jeremiah's Journey	JEREMIAH
104	Suffer Not in Silence	LAMENTATIONS
108	Shepherd Janitorial Services	EZEKIEL
112	Faith on a Popsicle Stick	DANIEL
116	A Call to Love	HOSEA
119	Oh, Mercy Me!	JOEL
122	Love Different	AMOS
126	Road to Redemption	OBADIAH

131	Me, an Author?	JONAH
135	Dear Hopeful	MICAH
138	Pass the Pepper	NAHUM
142	God, I'm Mad at You!	HABAKKUK
147	Happy Father-Filled Day	ZEPHANIAH
151	A Glorious Temple	HAGGAI
157	A New Generation	ZECHARIAH
161	Trust and See	MALACHI
166	Why Pray?	MATTHEW
170	I'll Pray for You	MARK
174	Thanks for the Burnt Bacon	LUKE
178	Made Known	JOHN
182	Evangelist: Age 6	ACTS
188	Divide and Conquer	ROMANS
193	Treasured	1 & 2 CORINTHIANS
197	Petals from Heaven	GALATIANS
201	Immeasurably More	EPHESIANS
208	Aloha	PHILIPPIANS
212	Who's Your Daddy	COLOSSIANS
216	The Gratitude Game	1 & 2 THESSALONIANS
220	The Timothy Award	1 & 2 TIMOTHY
224	Creative Correction	TITUS
230	Brown Paper Packages	PHILEMON
233	My Terrific Mom	HEBREWS
237	Rachel's Faith	JAMES
240	New Hope	1 & 2 PETER
244	A Boy and His Papa	1,2,3 JOHN
248	You Brought Jesus to a Bar?	JUDE
252	Life Assurance	REVELATION

IT'S REAL
to me

 INTRODUCTION

This book has been on my heart to write since 2001. Initially, I wanted to write a parenting book about God's presence in my life as a young mom.

But then I went back to teaching and wanted to share stories about what God was doing in my classroom.

But then my youngest son became a professional actor and I wanted to share stories about God using us on set.

But then I went on a mission trip to Africa and wanted to write about that amazing experience.

But then I experienced a miscarriage and wanted to bring hope and healing to others by how God had used my baby's little life.

But then I got divorced and my heart shifted to want to write about God in the midst of such devastation.

But then my dad died suddenly and I wanted to write a book commemorating him.

But then I became a full time caregiver to my handicapped mom and wanted to write about relying on God's strength, when called to care for your own.

But then I helped Mom sell our house that Dad built 50 years ago and together we started a whole new life in a whole new land, and I wanted to write about God's guidance in that.

So here I am 20 years later in 2021 and God has shown me a way to write about all of it in one book. *It's Real to Me* is a collection of stories from my life told through Scripture. Whether it's a passage, theme, or person from that particular book in the Bible, I see that God has used my trials to grow me, bless me, and launch me forward. My goal is not just to be an encouragement through my personal stories, but also to inspire others to make God's Word real in their own journey, and to find His mercies amidst the messes of life.

20/20 VISION

While the Bible is written somewhat in chronological order, this book is not. As I read **God's Word**, I recall random events and circumstances from my past that closely relate to a particular parable, person, or plight I see in Scripture. So, while I've kept God's Books of the Bible in order, you will find that my life is not. Think of this book as meeting a new friend; you learn things about each other naturally, as they come up. Over time you are able to put all the pieces together and you understand the bigger picture. So here we go. I'm Kimberly, nice to meet you! Let me tell you why the Bible is very real to me …

I grew up in a loving home and attended the little Lutheran school down the street from our house on the outskirts of Los Angeles County. I LOVED going to Sunday School. Looking back, I think it was the stories from the Bible that kept me so engaged. Week after week, I couldn't wait to hear what would happen next.

I was about five years old when I initially heard the story of Abraham and Sarah, the couple who loved God and really wanted a baby. They kept praying and one day when they were very old, God blessed them with baby Isaac.

Then came the part of the story that caused me to feel uncomfortable and quite fearful. My Sunday School teacher read these words straight from the Bible:

God said: "Take your son, your only son Isaac, whom you love, and go to the land of Moriah and offer him there as a burnt offering on one of the mountains of which I shall tell you."

What? God wants Abraham to kill the very son he patiently prayed for? This is horrible! Why would God do that? He's supposed to love us and care for us. I don't want to hear about a god that would be so mean. I no longer wanted to listen to this story.

Even as adults, it's easy to give this same response: "I don't want anything to do with a god that lets such bad things happen!" But if I choose not to flee and stay in God's Word long enough, I learn there is more to the story. There is a lesson, a promise, or a provision that God had for each person in the Bible. He does the same for people today. The only difference is that our stories are still being written.

From the bottom of that mountain, Abraham had no idea what God was going to do. But he knew God's voice, so he obeyed anyway. He trusted God to the point of actually building an altar, arranging the wood, and binding his son Isaac to it. The saving grace that happened at the top of that mountain was not only a relief to Abraham, but also to Kindergartner Kim. God sent an angel to stop His devoted follower and then provided a sacrificial ram to take the place of Abraham's beloved son. I did not see that plot twist coming. God was testing Abraham's heart. Would he still trust God, even when it made no sense and would cause him great anguish? Yes. The answer was yes, he would faithfully still trust God.

I continued going to Sunday School and years later, I would see the beautiful parallel from this story, to the story of God giving His only Son whom He loved, to take the place for us. In high school, I was asked to become a Sunday School teacher. I enjoyed conveying the message that no matter how bad things got, God had a plan. And no matter how much the people from the Bible disappointed or turned away from God – He never stopped loving them or forgiving them. God has always had my attention, I knew and believed what He was capable of doing – all I needed to do was put my faith in Him.

I once heard a fabulous analogy, illustrating the difference between "believing" and "having faith." There was a tightrope walker who was performing for a group of spectators. After walking successfully across the rope from hundreds of feet in the air, he asked the crowd below, "Who believes I can do it again while pushing this wheelbarrow?" Everyone in the crowd cheered loudly, letting him know they all believed in him! He then asks, "Can I have a volunteer to get into the wheelbarrow?"

The Bible defines faith in:

Hebrews 11:1

Faith is confidence in what we hope for and assurance about what we do not see.

The spectators may have believed the acrobat could do it, but no one gets in the wheelbarrow unless they have faith that he can. When I know God as my ultimate leader, I know He will not let me fall. And because He's God, I can be sure there is something better for me when the wheelbarrow ride is over. I've heard others say, "The Bible doesn't really apply to me," or "I just can't relate." Hmmm. Have you read it? Disappointments, fear, confusion, grief, shame, rejection, messed up marriages, infertility, wayward children, the death of someone you love, sibling rivalry, parenting problems, losing your home, losing your job, starting over… and I'm not even out of Genesis yet.

The Bible is filled with concepts and experiences that are very real to me. In reading my stories, perhaps you may find the Bible is real to you too.

God used every single one of these documented events to teach, equip, and inspire generations to come. Not to say that these stories all have happy endings, but it's the ultimate ending I choose to focus on. The last 10 years of my life have been a series of wheelbarrow rides. I've made it through by clinging to the knowledge that while I couldn't see what was in front of me, my Wheelbarrow Driver could. It was during the hard times that I found my greatest peace by reading the Bible and holding on tightly to my faith. I trusted God, and His words got me through: stronger, wiser, and a better version of the woman He designed me to be. I'm still a work-in-progress, so don't expect perfection from me on this side of eternity. I just pray He uses me to share with you, His hand on my imperfect past. I think Joseph (the one who got thrown into a pit by his jealous brothers) says it best when he speaks to his sorrow-filled siblings in the very last chapter of Genesis:

Genesis 50:19-20
But Joseph said to them, "Don't be afraid. Am I in the place of God? You intended to harm me, but God intended it for good to accomplish what is now being done, the saving of many lives.

THIS MOVE WILL TAKE A MIRACLE

What always impressed me most about Exodus was how that little baby
floating in the basket grew up to free God's people from captivity and an evil
Egyptian king. **Moses was willing to obey God by leading the Israelites
out of Egypt, but Pharaoh was determined to keep them in.** God had to
intervene with devastating signs and wonders in order to get this seemingly
impossible task done and point His people in the right direction.

....

One of the hardest things I've ever had to do in my life was sell my
parents' home—the home I grew up in, the home my dad built for his bride
50 years prior with only a workshop full of tools and his own two hands.
Like Moses, I felt God leading me to move on. I had now been divorced
for four years, my sons were in college, and I was in desperate need for
a fresh start. Right after my marriage ended, I moved back into the house
that raised me. It had been my home from birth to college, the home that
always welcomed my return, and the foundational place that gave roots
to the woman I would one day become.

Moving back into my childhood home was meant to be temporary. But
when my dad died suddenly the second year I was there, I knew I had
to stay. I gave up teaching and took over for my dad, as the full-time
caregiver to my mom in a wheelchair. I told Mom I would stay and try
my best to care for her over the next few years. We agreed that once
my youngest son graduated high school, we would re-evaluate. (In all
honesty, Mom didn't think she would even live that long.)

The next two years were really hard, but they went by fast. Mom and I
would often reflect on how God had got us through and how strong we had
both become. My dad had maintained their home and yard meticulously.

We joked it was like Disneyland: Everyday there was a project to be done. He loved that, but me, not so much. It was an old house on a large property. Cleaning, repairing, maintaining, watering, the list went on.

There was so much to do in addition to fully caring for my mom. We eventually hired a gardener, a maid, and workers as needed, but it seemed that for every task accomplished, another would reveal itself. How my dad managed to do all this year round, on his own, still baffles me.

Mom and I bonded during our time together and had an open dialogue about what would happen once it was time for me to move on.

We figured there were really only three options:

1. She could move to an assisted living facility. She and Dad had saved and invested their money wisely, and we could find her one that would feel like being on vacation everyday.

2. She could stay in her beloved home, and have caregivers come in around the clock.

3. She could come with me, and we could move on together.

In the summer of 2018, she had confidently made up her mind. "I want to go with you," she said. "This house just isn't the same without your dad and at this point, I just need a nice window to look out of." The idea of sifting through four generations of accumulated stuff was overwhelming to me. But my newly developed muscles from the last five years of hardships gave me the strength and perspective to forge ahead. I hired a highly recommended real estate agent whom I already knew from church. Bob was not only knowledgeable, but was also like a protective big brother ready to walk alongside and speak for us to get us through to the other side. I guess you could say he was the Aaron to my Moses. So Mom and I put the house on the market and began looking for our new beginning. To our surprise we got a full price offer four hours after the "For Sale" sign hit the dirt. Wow! This was going to be easier than I imagined!

We quickly started our search in Orange County where my sister and her family lived. Finding a one-story home that was updated, move-in ready, and with wheelchair accessibility proved to be a bit tricky. We also wanted to exercise my mom's right to Proposition 60/90, which stated that she could take her property tax amount with her, as long as the home she purchased was of equal or lesser value to the one she sold. As my parents purchased their home in 1967, for a whopping $25,000, the savings was considerable.

With a full price offer on our house and in escrow, we knew our parameters and felt confident we could find our new home within them. After two weeks of searching, we had a couple worthy contenders.

We were just waiting for our buyer to follow through on his down payment obligations before making an offer on a new house. He was dragging his feet and asking for more time. Being curious about this stranger, I went to the place everybody goes to in order to find out more: Facebook. I got his name off the escrow paperwork and typed it into the search bar. I found his page and despite not being his *friend* I could still see all his posts. The top one read: Property for sale in Tarzana, ½ acre lot, contact me for more information. He also listed the price for $50,000 more than we were asking. What a jerk! No wonder he was dragging his feet. He was waiting for his own buyer, he was merely the middle-man making a profit from our listing.

In the book of Exodus we learn of 10 plagues that curse the Egyptians and serve as hardships each time the King of Egypt changes his mind about allowing Moses to set the Israelites free. We too experienced a set of hurdles in attempting our own exit to a new land.

Plague #1: A Shyster!

We pulled out of escrow, let the potential properties go in Orange County and started over with trying to sell our house. After a successful open house we had a new offer on the table and quickly began this process again. With slightly less money to work with, we started our search once more.

Plague #2: An Empty Swimming Pool

The small swimming pool my dad had dug and built in our backyard when my sister and I were ages 5 and 9, had now been empty for 15 years. The bank would not approve the loan for our buyer unless it was filled and properly working.

Plague #3: A Weak Foundation

During the routine inspection process, the gentleman hired to asses the safety and condition of the house couldn't finish the job. He took one look at the foundation under the house and declared, "A lot of work and a specialist is needed."

Plague #4: A Drastic Price Drop

While the foundation may have been compromised and there were some structural issues to deal with, the buyer did not want to let the house go. The architectural talent and unique woodworking throughout the 2,800 square foot, ranch-style house was what made this property special. He was willing to continue on with the sale if we dropped the price considerably.

Plague #5: A Weak Selection

Our goal in all this was not to sell our house for lots of money, but to get a house for a house. This was my prayer: *Lord, just bring us a house that meets all of Mom's needs that we can easily exchange for this one.* The high price tag properties in the O.C made our new price range more challenging to work with. Most of what we could now downsize to would need to be a fixer-upper. This was not the idea of the new beginning we had set our sites on.

Plague #6: A Sinking Foundation

The specialist came out to assess the foundation and found that the soil was weak and while there was no immediate danger, the house would need to be "shored up" to keep from sinking over time. This was catastrophic news for the buyer. Lifting parts of the house up and stabilizing the foundation is not only expensive, but as concerning as it sounds.

Plague #7: Bye-Bye Buyer

This project just became too costly and involved for our buyer, as much as he originally wanted to hold onto the house. He was out. Thankfully, there were two business partners waiting in the wings who wanted to tear down the house and build a number of homes on the property. As much as this broke our hearts, we could see no other way.

Plague #8: Two Different Plans

It was now almost November, the holidays were approaching and fewer houses were being listed for sale. My sister started looking at assisted living facilities as a potential option. Her kids were still young and her husband traveled quite a bit, so while closer, she still wouldn't have as much flexibility to care for Mom. Our mom was basically paralyzed from the waist down, so the type of outside care she would need was going to be very expensive. In addition, she did not want strangers caring for her so intrusively. I began to realize that I would continue to be her primary caregiver, but with a pricey ocean breeze.

Plague #9: A Zoning Issue

About two weeks into escrow with our new buyers, they learned that our property was zoned for a maximum of three homes. This no longer made economic sense for them to use the property for their purpose.

Plague # 10: Three Strikes- You're Out!

Three months on the market, three times in escrow, and three times fallen out of escrow. I'm done.

I went to my ever-so-patient realtor, ~~Aaron~~ I mean Bob, and told him to take the house off the market. I was tired, depleted of hope, and needed the bleeding to stop.

He looked at me with understanding and said, "~~Moses~~ Kim, don't lose heart. If God wants this house to sell, it will. Keep praying, and trusting in Him. When you find the home He has for you and your mom, He will make it crystal clear and nothing will get in the way of Him blessing you."

(To be continued in "Numbers")

Exodus 14:13

Moses answered the people, "Do not be afraid. Stand firm and you will see the deliverance the Lord will bring you today.

IMAGE MANAGEMENT

Like many of the Old Testament books of the Bible, "holiness" is symbolized by physical perfection. Specific instructions are given on building altars to offer up **gifts of first fruits** to God. There are also guidelines for **sacrifices of atonement** using animals without blemish to bring as burnt offerings. While this is not something I can easily relate to in my own offerings to The Lord, this book of the Bible is full of symbolism, and I find that both applicable and relatable.

....

Symbolically, I had built an altar in my marriage. It resembled more of a Jenga tower (the game where you build a strong tower by overlapping a series of three wooden blocks atop one another). There was a point where I thought, "Wow, what we built is quite sturdy. This marriage is unbreakable!"

Then slowly and subtly, life's trials happen and with each unresolved hardship, a block is removed, compromising the firm foundation. I made attempts to fill the cracks in our structure with suggestions of counseling, marriage retreats, and couple's Bible studies, hoping desperately that we could grow in wisdom and benefit from structural support, and in addition have  accountability outside of ourselves. But being **unequally yoked** meant that our foundation would be shaky. For us, it would only be a matter of time before our marriage altar would come crashing down.

I, too, had played a critical part in removing blocks. I somehow convinced myself that if I believed the altar could remain standing (even without maintenance), it would. For me, divorce was never an option. I took "until death do us part" seriously.

Perhaps that false sense of security added to the weakening of our structural foundation. My husband deemed our altar unrepairable. He felt it would be easier to knock it down and start fresh with another one. His reasoning was, "I can't be married to a Super Christian. I feel guilty all the time around you. We fight about everything. I'm just not happy." I pleaded with him that we seek counseling, and eventually he agreed to go one time with me and one time without me.

In the Old Testament, priests were counted on to guide people in the right moral direction. My Christian therapist symbolized this role for me and his instructions were clear, "You need to let your husband go." I was shocked. "You came highly recommended by my church and by friends whose marriages you supposedly 'saved'," I said. "I hired you to do the same for us." The marriage family counselor explained that after several sessions with my husband and me, together as well as individually, he had reached the unfortunate conclusion that my husband's issues were so much deeper than our marriage. Although briefly touched upon, my husband refused to go any deeper, and in his mind, he had already decided to move past it.

It's impossible to help someone who doesn't want help. There was a part of me that felt relieved that I was being freed from this uphill battle, but in the depths of my heart, I still loved my husband. The only hope I had was that perhaps by divorcing he would no longer have my faith to lean on and he'd be forced to find his own faith. I was willing to live the next 40 years of my life without him if it meant the possibility of living in Eternity with him.

On December 29, 2012 - exactly one year after we separated - our marriage of 18 years, 7 months, and 16 days, was legally over. Sealed and delivered in a large manila envelope. Seeing the official stamp on a document that divided up all of our accumulated blocks into "his" and "her" piles was a strong dose of reality that our game had ended. Reading these new instructions on how time once spent together as a family would now be divided, broke my heart. Despite my signature on the dotted line, it was not the path I had chosen...yet clearly the one I was on.

On top of the sadness, I was embarrassed. Divorce. I've never liked the word. I've never had a heart for those who seemingly gave up on their marriage, and I never thought it would happen to me. I had painted such a pretty picture for others to look at. "Image management," is the term I found to best describe this. I remember one of our friends telling me, "Wow, if your marriage can't make it - what hope do the rest of us have?" I guess I managed to convince all but one person that our relationship was worthy of keeping. What I had brought to our marriage altar was no longer an acceptable offering.

I tried to console myself by thinking there would be no one else out there who would be willing to offer up the kind of sacrifices I did in our marriage. But within minutes of our separation, my (not yet) ex-husband already had a girlfriend. Eight months later, when our divorce was final, they were still together. I went from consoling myself to beating myself up. Clearly, I must be the broken one: Here I sit alone, devastated by all past, present, and future losses. Yet he had moved on, and somehow found a lamb without blemish.

A few months later, I sat in a new Christian therapist's office, describing my (now) ex-husband in this callous way. Once I was done spewing out my hurt, I was sure she would feel pity for me. Instead she asked me, "What do you think your former husband sees in this woman?" I had been storing up facts in my head each time my sons came home and mentioned something about her in passing. So without skipping a beat, I answered, "She's from Brazil. She dresses like a model. She works for a skincare company, so not only is she a working professional, but her face and body are flawless. She is younger than me. She has the daughter that my ex always wanted, and she makes everyone waffles on Sunday mornings."

Geez! Why would this therapist ask me that? By the time I got through my list, I felt worse and never wanted to come back to her office again - until I heard her follow up question: "Now tell me, what do you think God sees in you?" Before I could answer, I started to cry. I knew that God looks on the heart. And while I elevated those traits in this other woman, God didn't care about any of them. (Except maybe that she was kind enough to make people breakfast). The point is, I now understood what my new, wise therapist was doing. As I listed my own traits of trust, obedience, faithfulness, commitment, loyalty, and love, **I realized I had such great gifts to offer. Gifts fit for a King, not a quitter.**

We can't control our circumstances. But we can control who we are and how we will behave within the confines of them. I would have stayed and done whatever was needed to not break our family apart. I see now that God released me from a marriage that would have meant sacrificing the woman God designed me to be. And that's not a sacrifice that would be pleasing unto the Lord.

Leviticus 26:13
I am the Lord your God, who brought you out of Egypt so that you would no longer be slaves to the Egyptians; I broke the bars of your yoke and enabled you to walk with heads held high.

JOURNEY TO THE LAND OF PROMISE

In the book of Numbers, God's people are led out of Egypt. But instead of responding in **faith and obedience** when the journey gets tough, they are unbelieving and ungrateful towards God. This act of rebellion causes them to lose the **fulfillment of the promised land**, at least in their lifetime.

....

After nearly three months of trying to sell our home and enduring obstacle after obstacle, it was now November. Thanksgiving and Christmas were just around the corner, and this time of year is considered the worst to buy and sell. In addition, this month would have been my parents' 50th wedding anniversary, which seemed to add salt to our fresh wound. I felt so depleted and defeated. All I wanted to do was take care of my own, just like my dad had done for so many years. He made it look easy. He would always say, "I built this house to last a lifetime." I now understood that he meant *his* lifetime.

It had been almost three years since his unexpected death. I tried so hard to maintain our precious family home he had built with his own two hands. But I was mentally and physically exhausted. Staying in this house was no longer an option for me, or Mom for that matter. We would rather leave now, while our memories of the past were still fresh and happy. Despite pulling our house off the market, I would still go on the MLS every night and look for a new home that would meet our needs. I didn't expect to find much, but I didn't want to give up hope. Mom and I both wanted to move out of Los Angeles County and go somewhere with cooler temperatures and a small town vibe. We had exhausted our Orange County options, so I expanded my search the other direction. Ventura County was just 30 minutes away and it was cooler, quieter and less expensive.

As I swiped through the listings, I came across one house that was too good to be true. In the hundred homes we must have considered in the O.C., I never saw one as perfect as this one: It had hardwood floors throughout and wide hallways with an open floor plan, ideal for Mom to move about freely in her wheelchair.

Although it was a two-story home, it had two bedrooms and two bathrooms downstairs. Which was quite rare. This way Mom could have her own handicapped-accessible bathroom and the guest bathroom could be just that. The separate living area upstairs would be ideal for me to have my own space, as well as a fourth bedroom for my boys whenever they come home from college to visit.

This new find had only been on the market two days and there was going to be an open house that Saturday, on November 10. I knew I had to see it. Unfortunately, obstacles continued to follow me as the 101 Freeway was completely shut down due to the Woolsey Brush Fire. But if God could part the Red Sea for Moses, I was pretty sure He could clear a path out of the San Fernando Valley for me. I was able to take the long way around and use backroads. I didn't have a miraculous staff like Moses, but I was equipped with my dad's 2013 Toyota Camry, and it seemed to get the job done just as well. I made it right on time to the open house, and it was everything I hoped it would be. There were lots of people looking at this house and I began to feel overwhelmed. I heard the real estate agent tell someone else that they would start taking offers at the end of the weekend and would make a decision by Wednesday or Thursday. He then added, "This one is going to sell fast." After hearing that, I walked out. "Who am I kidding, I can't act fast," I thought. After all, our family's house wasn't even on the market anymore. Plus, I didn't even know if my mom would truly be willing to move out there. I drove off feeling so disappointed. That house really felt like it was made for us.

I drove around the adorable neighborhood with well-manicured lawns and evidence of happy active families throughout. I followed the beautifully paved sidewalks and learned there was a quiet little park at the end of the street. I found a shady spot, pulled the car over, and began to pout. Why would God bring me over hills full of hurdles, just to dangle this Promised Land in my face? (Sound familiar?)

I thought back to what our realtor (Bob/Aaron) told me, "If God wants this house to sell, it will. Keep praying, and trusting in Him. When you find the home He has for you and your mom, He will make it crystal clear and nothing will get in the way of Him blessing you." In that moment, I realized I had a choice: I could drive back to the Valley and just like the Israelites, wander about for the next 40 years. Or I could trust wholeheartedly that God could possibly be trying to bless me. I whipped the car around and drove back to the open house. The listing agent had just said goodbye to a couple in the doorway as I walked up the path.

"Hi Chris, my name is Kim," I said. "I know this open house is probably over, but would you mind if I took one more look?" I asked.

"Sure, not a problem," he said. "It's good you came back. Now you have the place to yourself." I took that as an encouraging comment.

As we strolled around the beautiful pinch-me-I-must-be-dreaming house, I began to tell Chris my story. I could just see my boys rolling their eyes at me, scolding "Mom! Strangers don't want to hear about your life story!" (Funny, if my sons only read one paragraph in this whole book, I hope it's this one that strangers are now also reading. <insert emoji with tongue sticking out>)

Well boys, I can't speak for others, but it turns out this stranger was very moved by my story. He shared that he too is a Christian, and graduated from UCSB with the youth pastor who currently owns this house. I told him my younger son was currently a freshman at UCSB and it turns out this realtor and Ryan both lived in the same dorm and had the same major! I'm not usually one to look for "signs," but when I'm desperately praying and seeking clarity, I cling on to the little things. And this house was full of little things that made me think God wanted me to live and care for Mom here.

As Chris walked me out, he said the owners were moving to Texas (coincidentally where my older son lives) and needed to be out of the house by December 30. The house was priced to sell, and after today, he expected multiple offers. If we wanted to make an offer on the house, we would have to have it in by Tuesday night, along with a personal letter introducing ourselves to the owners stating why we wanted to buy this house. I knew the writing part would be easy for me, but getting my mom on board with this crazy leap of faith idea … I'll leave God in charge of that one.

Numbers 33:53

Take possession of the land and settle in it. For I have given you the land to possess.

THE GIFT OF THE SABBATH

The book of Deuteronomy contains The Ten Commandments. I have grown to understand that these rules given by God are not to exercise power over me, but to show **His deep love for me.** Choosing to obey these rules is the way I show my deep love back to Him. But I can only truly experience this love when my **obedience comes from my heart,** rather than my head.

....

Driving to church (alone), trying not to be bitter that my boys declined to join me, I tuned into Christian radio, in hopes of changing my attitude. A song titled, "Back to You" by Mandisa came on and did the trick. *"It's not about what I do for You, it's about what You've done for me."* I love that line! I may not have been able to get my teenagers out of bed to go to church, but that wouldn't impact God's ability to bless my morning with Him.

After this "check-up-from-the-neck-up," I entered God's house, ready for whatever He had prepared for me. While still in the church lobby, I bumped into a woman I knew. With just a glance, I could tell she had been carrying around a heavy heart. As we chatted, she opened up to me about her marriage being a 'sham,' and wanting more, and feeling ready to walk away. Now that I'm divorced, it seems as if people feel I will be one to encourage the dissolution of their own marriages. I always tell them, "I would have taken a miracle over what our family went through and the consequences that ultimately came from that decision." Today I added, "We happen to serve a God of miracles, and while my marriage couldn't be restored, don't be too quick to dismiss God's hand on yours." Thankfully, I thought to mention the upcoming six-week sermon series on the topic of marriage that begins next Sunday at our church. A smile came across her face as we hugged and I said a quick prayer with her before going into the sanctuary.

Church that morning was awesome. The sermon was all about forgiveness, and again, "What He has already done for me." I then entered into my volunteer shift in the kids department, where a large group of adorable three-year-olds awaited me. One boy cried on and off throughout the hour, needing extra TLC and constant reminding that "Mommy is coming back." Despite the dried tears on his cheeks when his parents returned, they were grateful. This was the first church service they were able to sit through together, without one of them being called out to come and get him. I encouraged them that little Liam would get more and more used to the routine, that they should definitely keep coming as it would get easier and easier each week. All three of them walked out with smiles on their faces that mirrored mine. I fondly remember bringing my own little boys to Sunday School. Oh, how I wished it was still as easy as strapping them into a car seat and taking them wherever I wanted.

Before leaving church, I stopped by the information table to see if there were any additional diapers dropped off from last week's collection drive I had helped organize. There were about 10 more boxes and I offered to take them out of their "arms" and into "Open Arms Pregnancy Clinic" that week. The busy church secretary was delighted and offered to call someone to help me load them into my car, but I was energized, so I declined. I brought my little Ford Focus around to the front of the church, wondering if I would even be able to make them all fit. As I got out of my car, I heard a teenage girl arguing with someone on her cell phone. With her skateboard in hand, she was begging someone to please come get her, as it was now very hot and she didn't think she could "board" all the way home. Without hesitation, I walked up to her and said, "I'll make you a deal, if you help me load all these diapers into my car, I'll give you a lift to wherever you need to go." She smiled rather shyly, knowing I must have heard pieces of her unpleasant conversation, and then quickly agreed. Once my trunk and back seat were filled strategically with diapers, she grabbed her skateboard and squeezed into the front passenger seat.

As we drove, she shared with me that she was 17, and had been coming to Shepherd Church since she was four. At age five, she had to be put into foster care. Her current foster family didn't attend church, but allowed her to use her skateboard to ride down from their home in the hills of Porter Ranch to come to services. I again was reminded of my own 17- and 15-year-old who had chosen to not accept my ride to church. We seemed to have similar disappointments, but in reverse. I asked her if she still sees her biological parents. She explained that she was told that her mom was dead and that her dad was hiding from the police. Wow! What a weight for a child to bear. I was glad she had this church, and the desire to come. I know she's not my kid, but I was just so proud of her.

We reached her house and we thanked each other. She was grateful for the ride, I was grateful for the inspiration. It just so happens that she lived down the street from my old neighborhood. I hadn't been back to our family home since it sold after the divorce. Feeling armored up, I boldly decided to drive by. Seeing the house we lived in as a family of four for nearly a decade wasn't as sad as I thought it would be. God had filled my morning with blessings and as a result, I had a heart filled with joy.

Upon arriving back home, I learned that the two boys I left sleeping in their beds had been helping their Papa in the yard; sweeping leaves, cleaning out rain gutters, and filling up trash cans. In that moment, I was just as proud of them as I was of the other teenager I had met earlier that day.

There is something to be said about "just showing up" to the place God leads you and not bringing your own agenda. That morning, I had really wanted to use my "mom card" on getting the boys to come to church with me. But there was something in my heart that said, "Just let it go today." Now, in retrospect, I realize that if they had come, the morning would have panned out much differently…

- We most likely would have listened to their music on the way to church and I wouldn't have heard "Back to You."

- I would have merely said hi to my friend in the lobby, as my boys' presence would have deterred her from opening up about the trials in her marriage.

- Upon leaving church I would have never offered to take the diapers to "Open Arms," due to two passengers who took up much space.

- In turn, I would have never moved my car and overheard the girl's conversation. Neither she, nor the diapers, would have received transportation from me.

- Having not needed to drive up into the hills of Porter Ranch, I wouldn't have driven by our old house and been made aware of the healing that had occurred in my heart.

- Lastly, knowing the work ethic of my 83-year-old dad, the chores would have already been done by the time we got home. The beauty of his grandsons coming alongside to care for the yard (that we all are blessed to live in) would not have been experienced.

That morning I wanted to do the "right thing" for God, and make my boys go to church. But as Mark 2:27 says The Sabbath was made for man, not man for the Sabbath, meaning that it's His gift to us, not our gift to Him. Thank you Lord for orchestrating my Sabbath Day down paths I never would have known, had I ignored the prodding of my heart.

Deuteronomy 5:12
Observe the Sabbath day by keeping it holy, as the Lord
your God has commanded you.

THE WALLS CAME TUMBLING DOWN

Joshua was appointed by God to take over once Moses had died. He leads the Israelites into battle with the Canaanites, eventually entering the Promised Land. **Joshua pursues peace as he fights for God's people.** Despite bitter realities along the way, **Joshua trusts that God will deliver**.

One of the first Bible verses my oldest son, Blake, ever memorized was **Joshua 1:9.** When I came across the verse on a wall decal, he graciously let me buy it to put it up in his bedroom.

These were the words that the Lord spoke to Joshua as He commissioned His new leader to take control. Today it's a widely quoted verse, and from a young age, Blake deemed it his favorite.

During the first month of middle school, Blake turned 13-years-old. While having a September birthday often made him older than many of his classmates, in junior high this proved to be valuable. Having a little more maturity in a pond with fellow tadpoles, all morphing and developing simultaneously, gave him a leg-up, so to speak. He was serious about his commitments, and did well with managing schoolwork and his soccer schedule. If he had an assignment due Thursday, he would start it Tuesday night. He didn't want his Wednesday night soccer practice to get in the way of getting it done (yep, waiting a year to start Kindergarten was the right choice for him).

I remember when he had his first big middle school assignment. The sixth grade history students were to write a five-paragraph essay giving their personal opinion on how King Tut died. Blake worked on this report for hours, days before it was due. I was impressed. And as his homeschool teacher for the last two years, I was anxious to see how I (oops) how he would score.

He came home from school a few days later, frustrated and dumbfounded. He said the teacher called him and James up to her desk after class and held up their two essays, "Would either of you gentlemen like to explain to me how your papers are exactly alike, word for word?" Blake said he was shocked and couldn't speak. James on the other hand quickly spoke up and said, "I don't know, that's my work." When the teacher asked Blake if he wrote it himself, he told her," I promise you, I did." Blake told me that in that moment he didn't even consider that James was lying. Blake actually wondered if having similar interests and being so much alike, made their essays seem identical. Because neither of them 'fessed up to cheating she told them that they both had to rewrite the essay. Blake was so confused. He later remembered that in study hall, the day before the essay was due, James asked Blake if he had started the assignment. Blake told him he finished it already. James asked if he could see it, to know how to set up the heading. Blake agreed, but was focusing so hard on getting his math done before soccer practice that he didn't pay much attention. The bell rang and he grabbed his paper back and left.

Well, that night, Blake stayed up until 10 p.m. rewriting the paper he had already written. He was annoyed, but got over it quickly. I, on the other hand, did not get over it. I gave my son explicit instructions to no longer hang out or be friends with James.

"Mom, that's not gonna happen. I have every class with him and he's on the sixth grade soccer team with me," was his chill-out response.

"Well, he lied and cheated and took advantage of you. Plus, he had no problem taking full credit for your work when confronted by the teacher," came my heated reply.

Blake said he would be careful around James and never give him an opportunity to cheat off him again, but that they were still going to be friends and teammates. I understood, but the momma-bear in me was not happy about it.

Three weeks later, Blake came home from school and shared another incident that involved James. From the mere mention of that boy's name, my walls went up. I was already angry. The words "I told you so" were on the tip of my tongue and ready to go.

Blake's story went something like this:

> During English class today, James was excused to use the restroom. When he came back, he told me, "Blake, there's an eighth grader in the boy's room who just asked if I wanted to buy some drugs." James hesitated to go into the office and tell the principal because he was scared the eighth grader would find out and he'd get beaten up. I told James I would go with him, because what if the next sixth grader he asks says yes?
>
> James agreed, and I walked with him to the office. The principal handed James a yearbook from the year before and asked him

to try and find the boy's photo. James identified him straight away. The principal shook our hands and thanked us for being so courageous.

That afternoon, the eighth grade boy's name was announced over the loud speaker and he was called to the office. We later learned that the eighth grader had already been on probation before, and now he would be expelled given the school's "Zero Tolerance Policy" when it came to drugs.

Needless to say, my walls came tumbling down as I realized how wrong the advice I gave my son was. If he doesn't talk to James anymore, who does James go to when he gets offered drugs in the boy's room? The possibilities are infinite. But I doubt any of them end better than this one does. I wondered if being homeschooled and distanced from peer pressures the last few years made Blake's response different from James' response to this. Regardless, I knew right then and there that as a parent, I could only do so much to protect my children from the evils of this world. By age 13, I'd given him roots, and was now being forced to give him wings. At times I'd get discouraged. Am I capable of following God's command in Joshua 1:9, to be strong and courageous and unafraid of the many dangers my kids will face? But then I think, if God's going to give me a command, He's probably going to equip me to do it. So I backed up one verse to Joshua 1:8. It's a less popular verse that you probably won't find a pre-made wall decal for, but equally just as important.

Joshua 1:8

Keep this Book of the Law always on your lips; meditate on it day and night, so that you may be careful to do everything written in it. Then you will be prosperous and successful.

A GAL LIKE GIDEON

God had delivered His people, the Israelites, out of captivity and into an established land that they did not have to toil, build, or work for. With this, they promise to serve and worship the one true God... but they don't. The Book of Judges is a continuous cycle of the Israelites' disobedience and disregard for the Lord. God hand-picks individuals to act as judges to rise up and steer the Israelites back on track. An angel of the Lord appears to Gideon and tells him to **go, in the strength he is given, and save Israel from the enemy's hands**. Despite his love and fear of the Lord, Gideon questions and doubts if he's really the one God wants to use. Gideon politely asks the Lord again and again to prove Himself by showing him specific signs. God graciously performs these mini miracles, to ease Gideon's doubts and fears.

....

There have been a number of times in my own life that I have asked God to show me if what I am being asked to do is really from Him. It's not that I doubt His ability to do great things in my life, I'm just not always sure it's His voice I'm hearing.

In 1998, I was five years into my marriage, with a one-year-old baby and a husband who had just been laid off from his job. I left teaching to be a stay-home-mom, and I was happy in my new role. My husband was given a severance package, and the plan was to stretch it out until he found another full-time position. During this time, a buddy invited him to a sales pitch meeting for a pyramid-style business venture. We both agreed before he went that he would NOT buy into this. He was just going to fill a seat and support a friend.

When he came home that night overly excited and smiling like he struck gold, I got worried. Thankfully, he prefaced the conversation with, "There is no way we are signing up to sell that stuff." Phew! So what could he possibly be so happy about? He went on to share that the meeting was held at a tutoring center. As he sat for two hours in a classroom type environment and read the writing on the walls, an idea began to grow. He could use his business/accounting background, and I could teach part-time. It made perfect sense to him that we start up our own tutoring center.

Oh my! I would rather have revisited the pyramid scheme. At least that's a business already in place and the accountability factor is built in. Starting our own business, from scratch, with a baby on our hip, seemed completely irresponsible. I didn't want to squelch his excitement, but I hated the idea. I suggested we sleep on it and pray on it. I went to bed and he stayed up most of the night planning a way to make this idea work.

I woke up to a pad of lined paper filled with notes waiting for me at the breakfast table, along with an energetic sales presentation. He had researched the location of all the schools in the San Fernando Valley, cross-checked them with locations of conflicting businesses and pinpointed upper middle class communities that could afford outside tutoring. He then brought out the Thomas Guide, which showed individual dots representing his research. (I'm not going to lie; it was impressive.) I then noticed one dot in the center that was larger than all the rest. Come to find out, this dot represented the perfect location to open our presumed establishment. It was a small two-story business center, next-door to a library. He already reached out to the landlord and as soon as I finished my Cheerios and packed up the diaper bag, we would all head over there to check it out.

Clearly the situation had ramped up overnight and I had no other choice but to pull a "Gideon" and prayed, "Lord, if this is something that is truly for us, You are going to have to literally pave a yellow brick road for me. It needs to be easy to walk on and obvious in its direction. I need to know You're in this as much as my husband is... because I'm not feeling it at all."

We left from our townhouse in Northridge and pulled into the parking lot in under 10 minutes. *Location-check.

There was a sign that indicated a vacancy for lease. *Availability-check.

It was on a busy street but had plenty of customer parking spaces. *Visibility and accessibility-check, check.

The owner of the building was waiting outside for us and gave us a warm and friendly greeting. *Landlord-check.

While giving us a tour, the connection was made that we went to high school with this man's son. The three of us all graduated Class of '89 together. Suddenly, this landlord viewed us as family and became emotionally invested in our endeavor. He dropped the down payment in half and took 30% off our monthly rent. *Affordability-check.

We told our new relative we would get back to him after doing some more homework. We still had the matter of filling the space with furniture and educational supplies. Oh, yeah, and students. We would need those too.

We told our friends and family about the idea and they were all encouraging. Even my wise, conservative dad was on board. He offered his skills as a master carpenter to build desks for the center. My parents also happily volunteered to babysit their grandson whenever we needed. *Outside support-check.

After finding chairs, computers, and educational resources for a steal at Costco, all that was left was advertising. My husband's father owned a printing company and offered to print up all our mailers and forms at no cost. He even threw in custom pencils, magnets, and bookmarks. I still had a school roster from teaching to send to 250 families that already knew me. One of the moms of a former student gave me the roster from her daughter's new school to send out to 300 additional families (both were within a five-mile radius of the tutoring center).

We called "Uncle Landlord," signed the paperwork and put all of these wheels in motion. We were able to pay for everything plus first month's rent with the severance money from my husband's former job. God, You amaze me! *Yellow brick road-check.

The week before we were scheduled to open our doors, my doubts crept back in. We had sent out tons of mailers and were getting in-quisitive phone calls, but still didn't have any sign-ups. So, I prayed like Gideon once more. "Lord, you have been so faithful in answering my prayer and giving me your clear blessing over all of this. I'm sorry to question You. But my two most important jobs are as wife and mother. I don't want to take time away from my child to sit in an empty room, resenting my husband for thinking his plan would succeed. I'm scared that after all this, nobody will come. Please do something big to show me that You're still in this with us. Amen"

That evening my husband and I went to our weekly Bible study meeting. Instead of having it at our usual location, our friends suggested we all meet at the new tutoring center and pray over it together. I didn't see the difference between praying there or in their living room, God hears our prayers either way. But we were happy to have the people who were lifting our leap of faith up in prayer week after week, come and see our space.

Our small group loved what we had created. They were so encouraging and positive about it all. Everyone took a turn praying very specifically over every aspect of this new business and the people who would walk through those doors. It was such a beautiful act of love and support for us. Both my husband and I teared up. I wondered if this night was the "big thing" I had asked God for. As we were all leaving, our friend Jeff saw a stack of flyers on the front desk and asked if he could take some. He went on to say that there were a couple of people at his work with kids and maybe they would be interested. Jeff worked about an hour away from where our tutoring center was located, so I didn't expect anything to come out of it. Boy was I wrong! A few days later, I got a call from a mom whose son was in my fourth grade class. She said that her husband came home from work with one of our flyers that Jeff had handed him. I laughed and told her that I mailed her a flyer two weeks ago. She said she always throws junk mail away without reading it and tells me that her daughter is struggling so much in first grade that the teacher wants to hold her back next year. She wondered if little Chelsea could come everyday after school from 3:00 to 5:00 p.m. to catch up and grow in confidence. I was speechless. She went on to say that the money was not an issue, she was prepared to hire us for the rest of the year, if needed. She said she would rather spend the money now on catching her daughter up, than spend it on an additional year of private school tuition if Chelsea were to be held back.

With our first student signed up for 10 hours a week, her payment alone covered our monthly rent and expenses. Any student after that would be profit. Is there no end to how much God loves me? Thank you, Lord, for showing me in the little things that You are the Big Thing!

Update:

We ran a successful tutoring business for nearly two years, helping over
90 students in total. To help manage things, I went to my alma mater
and offered a paid internship to a few CSUN students who were getting
their teaching credentials. At the end of 1999, we gave birth to our
second son, Ryan, and my husband was offered a fantastic new job.
We moved the business to our new house and I continued to tutor, but
on a smaller scale. Oh, and Chelsea came to tutoring each day, and was
able to go on to second grade the following year.

WHERE YOU GO, I GO

My mom and I have a special attachment to the story of Naomi and
Ruth. It's a beautiful **story of redemption**. After her husband and two
sons die, Naomi decides to travel back to her home town and releases
her two daughters-in-law back to their families of origin, as well. But
Ruth insists on staying by her Mother-in-Love's side. Naomi's other
daughter-in-law also loved her very much, but did not feel the same
calling as Ruth did.

···

Much like this mother-daughter duo, Mom and I found ourselves without
husbands, living in a land that no longer felt like home. I too had a sister
who helped out immensely at the time of my dad's death, and from time
to time when she could break away. But she had an established life with
her husband and kids two hours away.

Many have asked me why I would choose to stay with my mom when
she had resources available for outside care. Perhaps it was because
I knew what it was like to have my true love leave and my life take a
tragic unexpected turn. My parents welcomed me home, no questions
asked, after my separation and divorce. Without giving it a second
thought, I wanted to be there for Mom too.

After years of mourning our lost loves in the home Dad built and in the
backyard where my wedding was held, we were both ready for some
new scenery. I drove home from touring our potential new home with
such peace. I truly believed God wanted to bless us and if this was to
be our house, He would make that happen. I told Mom all about my
last three hours and as the words left my lips, I realized how crazy I
must have sounded to her. She listened intently and looked over the
colorful presentation folder of the house and agreed that it really did
look perfect.

Well, if I am crazy, I clearly get it from my mother, as she told me to call our realtor Bob and see if it was even a possibility. The next thing I know, we had Bob putting our house back on the market, priced to sell, with an "as is" disclaimer. The house in Ventura County was considerably less than the ones in Orange County, so even with bringing our price down further, we were well within our "house for a house" swap-out-plan.

The next two days it poured down rain. We had a couple potential buyers come look at our house, and Bob set up an appointment for Mom to see the house in Ventura on Tuesday morning. The Monday before, she had four of her retired airline besties over for lunch. As we sat around the dining room table, Mom slid out the photo brochure of the Ventura house and began to gush to her friends. I was relieved that she was excited about this endeavor as I was. Her sharing was very bold and perhaps a bit premature. Still, I was interested in what her friends would say. These ladies have all known each other since they were in their twenties. They have always looked out for one another and would be honest in their opinions. To my surprise, they were unanimously ecstatic for us. They said the house was not only gorgeous, but also perfectly equipped for our current circumstances. Having their vote of approval only made Mom and I more confident about this possible venture out together.

On Tuesday morning, I lifted Mom into the car and we met Bob in Ventura for our own private showing. The 101 Freeway had reopened, but as we drove, the outside air gave off a stench similar to wet cigarettes. The recent rainfall on the blackened hillside offered a 4-D experience as we made our way through.

At one point, Mom made one of her witty comments, "Are you taking me to hell?"

"No, but we may have to go through hell to get there," came my quick comeback.

After 3 years of living together, we had developed a banter that seemed to keep us smiling. I was not about to let the wasteland to the left or to the right detour me. I kept my focus straight ahead, physically and spiritually. I knew when we got to the top of the grade, the view would look much different. And it did. We pulled into the quaint neighborhood and Mom was as giddy as I was. But once I got her out of the car and began to push her wheelchair up the driveway, she began to cry.

"What's wrong, Mom?"

"Did you see the address number?" her voice quiet and shaky.

I looked up to see the number 1168 affixed to the house.

"That's my wedding anniversary, November 1968," she explained.

Wow, God! Okay, never mind what I said four chapters back... I do believe in signs. I easily maneuvered Mom's chair through the doorway and she coasted right in. Having quite a bit of carpet in our current home, Mom practically floated as she rolled herself throughout the downstairs. Needless to say, it was a great tour. Mom asked blunt questions and both real estate agents were impressed by her wise discernment.

As we left, I asked Mom, "Was there anything at all you didn't like about this house?"

"Well... I didn't like that the dining room chairs had all white fabric on them. I don't understand how she keeps them clean with four children in the house," was her red flag response.

Seeing as that was the only thing she could come up with, I felt it was a hurdle we could get past. That night, I sat with my laptop at my dad's study desk, writing my letter to the owners (like us! - like us! - like us!), while my mom took on the brave task of calling my sister to tell her we were putting an offer on a house in the opposite direction of where she lived. I completely understand my sister's confusion. Spontaneously buying a house in a community where you don't know anyone and your family is now over two hours away, does sound irresponsible. But it wasn't a leap in the dark, it was a leap of faith; and to me those are very different. I was so proud of my mom as I listened to her calmly and confidently tell her youngest daughter, "This is what I really want."

That night, we submitted our letter and (slightly over asking price) offer to the powers that be. We had done our part, we trusted God, and now we would wait to see what happened. The next morning I got a call from my sister. She was hurt and angry that this was happening. "We haven't even sold Mom's house yet.... How can you put an offer on another one? Dad would never approve of what you're doing," she told me. She had a point. Plus our track record on this house hadn't been very good. Looking back, I think this was a test from God: Would I be willing to walk away from something I really wanted? I called Bob and told him I thought we needed to renege our offer. Bob heard me out and then said, "Let me ease your mind. I just got a full price offer on your house. I know you have three more potential buyers coming by today, but know that if they're interested, they'll have to get in line," he added. By that evening, Bob had learned that there were seven other offers on the house we wanted in Ventura and at least one was higher than ours. But the listing agent and current owners were really touched by our letter and our story, so they took the night to think about it. While Bob was on the phone telling me all of this, he got another call. It was the agent of someone who had looked at our house today. Her client wanted the house too, and it was another full price offer, but this time, all cash.

An all cash offer meant that we didn't have to fix the empty swimming pool, because there would be no bank loan. It also meant that we could pay cash for the house we wanted to buy, which was enough to cause the family in Ventura to confidently choose us over all the others.

Both escrows were 45 days, so we opened and closed escrow on the exact same days. We enjoyed our last Christmas in our family home and started the new year with a new beginning.

The story of Naomi and Ruth ends with Ruth meeting and falling in love with a man named Boaz. Mom and I have often joked about God finishing our story the same way. But recently, I reread the book of Ruth and came to realize something new. Boaz represents God's ability to provide and care for His people. So we already have our Boaz too, for God has brought us provisions in many other forms.

Ruth 1:16

But Ruth replied, "Don't urge me to leave you or to turn back from you. Where you go I will go, and where you stay I will stay.

LETTING GO

Samuel is first introduced in God's Word as a baby who was prayed for by his barren mother, Hannah. Her trust in the Lord is so immense that she vows if God will give her a son, she will **"give him to the Lord for all the days of his life"**. Hannah is revered in the Bible for having the strength to trust God in such a way to let go of her son at a very young age and allow him to be raised by another, so that Samuel would be able to serve the Lord to the fullest.

Growing up, Hannah's story helped me understand what it must be like for a mother to give her child up for adoption. Both value life as a gift and despite their struggles and efforts to bring such a life into this world, they are selfless enough to trust there is something more for this child than they can provide.

Little did I know that many years later, I would find myself in a position to love in a way I never thought I could. January 30, 2017 was the day I had my Hannah moment. My youngest son, Ryan, was newly 17 and I made the heart-wrenching choice to let him go from my care. He wanted desperately to leave his high school and community of friends and start fresh somewhere else. The idea of "Ryan starting fresh" sounded like an oxymoron. He was in the middle of his junior year at a private all-boys college preparatory high school. He was well respected as a leader on The Ambassador Team, and held a current G.P.A of 4.6. He was well-liked by the teachers, administration, and student body. He had a good group of friends that he hung out with during the school day. He performed at the top of his class and his teachers knew they could count on him to participate in class discussions. The college advisor on his campus believed in his success and was guiding him towards a scholarship to the university of his choice.

Despite possessing everything an eleventh grader should have as he looks towards applying to top colleges, he wanted to leave his school. I understood the last year had been a rough one; on top of being a child of divorce, he had also lost his beloved Papa, watched his brother move out of state for college, and gotten reprimanded a handful of times for "stupid teenage stuff." But he was still in a position to succeed and finish this last stage of childhood strong. As his mom, I believed in him and felt it was my job to see him through this. But he was of the opinion that this small private high school had too many rules - they were too strict, and he felt like a prisoner. Ryan's older brother had thrived in this environment, but my two boys were very different from one another. In the past year and a half, Ryan had made some poor choices with friends outside of school. These choices and behaviors trickled into his school environment and he had been held accountable. I was grateful that the administration held him to a higher standard. Ryan admitted to having issues with authority and continued to tell me, "I hate it there."

Actually, the summer before junior year, he had wanted to leave, but I refused to sign a release form. Per our divorce decree, both parents would need to consent to the child leaving their current school. Without my consent, Ryan would not be allowed to transfer to the school near where his dad was planning on moving. I wanted Ryan to have stability, and I didn't feel this move would provide that. Plus, he was doing so well academically during the toughest most crucial year of high school. As an educator and his mom, I thought good grades and leadership skills were the very things that defined a successful student. I was proud of all he had accomplished, despite his momentary lapses of better judgment.

My choices were simple: Do what I felt was best for my son, despite his lashing out. To continue to sit on him for the next year and a half, paying for him to go to a school he didn't appreciate, equipping him to get into a fancy college with an impressive scholarship, all while keeping him close to me so that I could try to keep him from screwing it all up. Or go against my desire as a mom to protect him and release him to do things his own way. To allow him to move 88 miles away, live full-time with his dad, and possibly fall flat on his face - giving up the "pretty paper trail" of all that he had accomplished.

I found myself praying constantly about this issue and never feeling a true peace either way. I wonder if Hannah felt at peace when she left Samuel with Eli. Perhaps the peace comes from recognizing that God has a plan and if we need to go through some uncertainty to relinquish our perceived control over to Him, then so be it. Sometimes doing something for a greater good makes no earthly sense. The truth is: It's not about what college Ryan goes to. It's about his self-discipline and the ability to be responsible in life. I would rather him go to a local community college and continue to figure himself out, than an Ivy League school with a scholarship and a sense of entitlement as he experiences a long-awaited freedom from the grasp of his mother.

No longer having the support and presence of a husband, nor my wise dad, nor my older son, made it harder to stand my ground when it came to "what I felt was best for my child." It was a daily uphill battle, but I willingly fought it for that first semester of Ryan's junior year. After Christmas Break, he returned to school, only to dislike it more. To paraphrase his words: This school has rules that squelch my individuality, it's too small and micro-manages its students. You not signing the release form is holding me hostage in a place I don't want to be.

I knew at that point I needed to let him go and figure it out for himself. Initially, it felt like giving in would be rewarding his teenage behavior, but I had a feeling there would be tougher lessons ahead and that my attempts to rescue him would only further enable him. His dad was moving out of the area, for no other reason than wanting a fresh start (sound familiar?). I begged him to please wait until Ryan graduated high school, but his mind was made up. Ryan adamantly wanted to go with him. There comes a time in a parent's journey when you have to realize that the battle is no longer yours to fight, that squishing your child into a safe, strong, healthy box is perhaps hindering him from truly figuring his life out. Truthfully, I was tired. For the last nine months I had stuffed his complaints aside and persevered with what I knew to be best. But then I began to think, how would he ever be able to make hard decisions in the future if I won't allow him to decide a few important things on his own right now? Knowing your child is important, and sometimes you can't parent all of your children the same way. Those who are visual or auditory learners can learn simply from listening to instructions or watching someone else go through something similar. But not Ryan. He has always been a kinesthetic learner; he needs to experience it for himself to truly understand the outcome.

My prayer was (and still is) that he proves me wrong, rises up despite the greater obstacles ahead, and remains the excellent student and leader on his own accord. That he does it for himself and not for anyone else. That his relationship with his dad grows even stronger, and decades from now, he looks back on this time and says, "It molded me into the man that God created me to be."

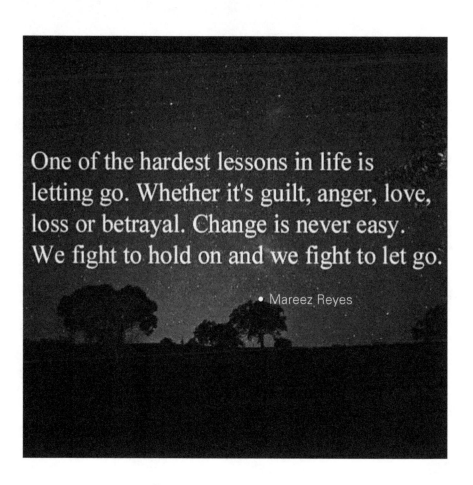

One of the hardest lessons in life is letting go. Whether it's guilt, anger, love, loss or betrayal. Change is never easy. We fight to hold on and we fight to let go.

• Mareez Reyes

1 Samuel 1:28

So now I give him to the Lord. For his whole life he will
be given over to the Lord.

TOUCHING ETERNITY

I love the story of the prophet Elijah bringing God's glory to a poor widow and her son on the verge of death, in the first Book of Kings. Elijah asks the woman for a piece of bread, but all that she has left to survive on is **"a handful of flour in a jar and a little olive oil in a jug."** She has accepted that this is all she has and is prepared to make one last meal of it and die. Elijah tells her not to fear, **the God of Israel will grow what little she has**. She acts in faith and there was plenty day after day to eat. What started as a minuscule amount becomes more than she has room to store. Some time later, her son becomes ill and stops breathing. God uses Elijah once again, this time to save the boy's life.

....

As you will read in chapters to come, God chose me to be the mother of a little life that would leave the palm of my hand, and then touch Eternity in a powerful way. While my baby, Jeremiah, was not able to live here on Earth, there is no end to his impact on this world. Here are a few things God has chosen to show me, on this side of Eternity:

- Thanks to God and Google, my baby's photograph and blog have thousands of views spanning across many countries.

- I have been asked by high school students, a number of times, if they may use my story and baby's picture to present at their school, in their pro-life speeches.

- In January 2014, I started a miscarriage support group where a dozen women, husbands, and even a grandmother were in attendance. Out of the 12, seven were new believers or wanting to rekindle their faith due to their miscarriage. Two of them were baptized after attending our small group Bible study.

- "In His Arms" miscarriage ministry has been offered at Shepherd Church since 2014. Sign-ups are ongoing throughout the year.

- I have lost count of the secondhand stories that have come to me, boasting God's healing power through Baby Jeremiah. One such story touched me deeply. With the sender's blessing, I have copied and pasted it below; just as it appeared in my message box on Facebook:

  I hope you remember me. I saw you at church tonight and I wanted to talk to you but the service was about to start. After church I couldn't find you. I just wanted to tell you a quick story. Because we have mutual friends on Facebook, I saw a comment one of my friends made to you when you lost your baby. I asked about what happened and I think she sent me a link to your blog and I saw the picture of your baby boy. I showed my girls (at the time 16 and 14) and used it as a way to talk to them about how babies are not just a blob of nothing, even at 12 weeks and how abortion is so wrong. We were fascinated at how developed he was and we cried when we read your story about him. Fast forward early November 2013, my now 17-year-old asked me about you and wanted to see Jeremiah's picture. I showed it to her. By the way, we just Googled it and there he was under 13-week old fetus. Anyway, a few weeks later did I get the shock of my life when she told me she was 3 weeks pregnant. My daughter seriously contemplated abortion out of fear and shame. Her biggest worries were that people at church would think I was a bad mother because she was pregnant and she was afraid her sister would be mistreated at school because of her pregnancy. Isn't it sad that the very places (church and

Christian schools) that tell us to be pro-life and that abortion is so wrong are the places that young girls fear will shun them the most? Thank God my daughter made the right decision and one of the turning points for her choice was Jeremiah's picture. Thank you for sharing your story because you saved my grandson's life. His name is most likely going to be Elijah but Jeremiah was what I would have named him if he were my son. Thank you again and God bless you.

My reply:

Thank you for sharing this with me. I am in tears over what God continues to do with this little life. Tomorrow will be 2 years since he came into our world and left an inspirational imprint. I can't wait to meet Elijah. I love that he will have the name of a powerful prophet, just as Jeremiah does. Well, I'm off to church, for the first time this weekend. Funny, that must have been an angel you saw last night, for I wasn't there. A reminder that God always makes a way for His stories to be told. I love hearing how God continues to use Jeremiah's life to impact this world again and again.

In 1 Kings 17, God used Elijah to help spare the life of a little boy. In my story, God used my little boy to help spare the life of Elijah. How awesome is that?!

2020 Update:

Elijah is now six years old.
Pictured here with his proud
mom and her loving husband.

BACK TO AFRICA

In 1 Chronicles, Chapter 17, David desires to build a temple in honor of the Lord that will house the Ark of the Covenant. This sacred chest that holds the Ten Commandments and serves as an important symbol to the Israelites that God is with them, was currently being stored under a temporary tent. David shares his idea with a fellow prophet and friend named Nathan. Nathan encourages David by saying, **"Whatever you have in mind, do it, for God is with you."**

....

Toni C. and I had only known each other for two years, but became fast friends due to our similar life circumstances. Both recently divorced, single in our 40s, with two teens each, and both with servants hearts for the Lord. From the moment I told her about my 2007 mission trip to Africa, she made me promise that if I ever went back, I would take her with me. She'd never been on a mission trip, and now that she was making her own decisions she was certain it was what she wanted to do.

When I was in Uganda in 2007, I met a teacher named Geoffrey who I held in high regard and I continued to communicate with via email for years after my visit. I would wire him money from time to time, to aid him in providing tuition for his younger siblings, who desired a higher education

 to become teachers themselves. He did not have a computer of his own, but would make his way to an internet café near his village to write to me about his family, his engagement, then marriage, and eventually the birth of his first child.

Early on he shared his dream of starting a primary school in the poor community of Tororo, Uganda where he grew up and where his parents still reside. I wanted to be a part of building this school and bringing hope to children who had such a great desire to learn, but whose days consisted mainly of trekking to a well or a swamp to gather water for their families.

I'll never forget the day that Geoffrey emailed me paperwork for a plot of land near his parents' home that he was hoping to purchase; an ideal spot for *God's Glory Nursery and Primary School*. I suppose Toni was to me like Nathan was to David. "If God's in it, go for it!" She was definitely my cheerleader and clearly had the gift of encouragement. Toni also wanted to help build this school. Twenty thousand dollars for an acre of land seemed like a reasonable amount, but two single moms sending that kind of money to a third-world country seemed crazy irresponsible. Toni and I both had money saved up from settlements given after the dissolution of each of our marriages. The idea of using money that came out of something so horrible to make a positive impact in the lives of others felt like an amazing opportunity. It wasn't until she said, "You give half and I'll give the other half," that I realized how impactful my testimonies of Africa had been. She went to her bank and got a cashier's check for $10,000. The teller behind the counter was skeptical and felt the need to warn Toni about the amount of fraud they see in transactions overseas. Toni thanked her for the warning and came to meet me in front of my bank. By the time she got to me, that tiny seed of doubt had grown. She asked if we could first get a coffee at Starbucks across the way. As we drank our comfort-seeking drinks, I reminded her that I have wired money numerous times from my account directly into the account that Geoffrey had set up at his bank in Uganda. I know that it is always safer to go through an organization when donating money, but I knew Geoffrey personally and after nearly seven years of continual communication and proof that he always used the money as stated, I knew it would get to him. I then added that if she was having second thoughts of investing this money in building the school, then she should not give me that check. She suggested we pray again about it. So right there on the Starbucks patio we poured our hearts out to the Lord, asking Him for wisdom, guidance, and clarity. We asked that this money be used only for His plan and for His glory. Praying that it would arrive in Geoffrey's Uganda account safely and that it would be used for buying the land and constructing the school. After about 10 minutes of concentrated back and forth conversational prayer, we both felt at peace to move forward as planned.

She handed me her cashier's check and we said goodbye in the parking lot. She left to pick up her son from school and I walked into my bank to wire our combined $20,000 to an account in Africa. As I went to push open the large glass entrance door, a tall African American man with a kind smile pulled the door open from the inside. I smiled back, and thanked him as he held the door open for me. He then looked straight into my eyes and said, "God's gonna answer that prayer." He continued out to the parking lot, as I continued into the bank. It wasn't until I got to my banker's desk that I actually processed what that man just said to me. I must have looked as shocked as I felt, because my usual banker, Kyle, looked up at me from his desk and said, "Ms. Preston, are you okay?" I then tried to explain to Kyle what just happened. As I spoke, I attempted to mentally connect how that man knew from inside the bank that we were praying outside, away from the bank. Even if he had somehow seen us, how odd that he was certain enough that it was me, and that he would boldly tell me that as our paths happened to cross. Kyle found it surprising too, and asked me what the man looked like. I got chills. What are the odds that I ask God for clarity on sending funds to Africa and this man brings the clarity I had just finished praying for?

Kyle didn't even remember seeing him in the bank, but I know I didn't imagine it.

I confidently wired the money and then called Toni, as well as emailed Geoffrey from my cell phone. They were both so touched by God's loving confirmation in this transaction. Their faith inspired me to stop trying to make sense of it and just trust that "God was gonna answer that prayer." Over the next nine months, the land was purchased and much of the school was built. In the Spring of 2015, Geoffrey asked us to pray for more provisions in this building project. The school still needed a roof, a play yard, and a latrine. Once those were in place, they would seek donations for school supplies and desks. I knew I could reach out to others and ask them for contributions, but they would have nothing other than my word as proof that this was a legitimate school – that I had never seen.

The only way to know for sure was to get on a plane and go and check it out. If I was going to testify to this school and ask others to partner and come alongside us to "raise the roof," I needed to speak first hand to its existence. So, I kept my promise to Toni and we booked a flight for September 2015 for a 10-day trip to Uganda. No organization to back us or protect us, just two single moms from Los Angeles, venturing out of our comfort zones and hoping to learn God's will for us and this school.

By the time we left we were prayed up and stocked up. Everyone we knew (and some we didn't know) had either donated items for us to take over or covered us in prayer, or both. Between the two of us, we had our allotted four checked bags full of school supplies and hygiene items, and managed to squeeze all our personal items into our carry-on luggage. Perhaps this level of excitement was similar to what David and Nathan felt in regards to building a temple for the Lord.

Although, 1 Chronicles 17 goes on to say:

But that night the word of God came to Nathan saying, "Go and
tell my servant David, 'This is what the Lord says: You are not the
one to build me a house to dwell in."

This was our prayer, that God would continue to make it so clear as
to what we should do or not do, that it would be as if we could hear
His voice.

1 Chronicles 17:19
Lord, for the sake of your servant and according to your will,
you have done this great thing and made known all these
great promises.

NOT OURS BUT HIS

A reoccurring theme in the Old Testament is **the Israelites' disregard for God**. Unfortunately, this is why the original temple was destroyed and God's people were exiled to Babylon for 70 years. When King Cyrus comes to power, **the Lord moves his heart** to allow the exiled Israelites to return to Jerusalem and rebuild God's temple. Construction of the new temple begins. While many rejoiced over the foundations of the House of the Lord being laid, those who were old enough to remember the earlier temple wept at the difference. People could not distinguish between the cries of joy and the cries of disappointment, as it was heard from afar.

....

The 19 hours of total air travel from Los Angeles International Airport to the tiny airport in Entebbe, Uganda gave us lots of time to think and pray about what we were about to encounter. We sent Geoffrey some money ahead of time to be able to rent a car and hire his friend, Martin, to drive us around. We disembarked the plane down a rickety staircase on the edge of the runway and walked inside. The entire airport appeared to be just one large room partitioned into areas for customs, visas and baggage claim. It had been seven years since I had last stood in this airport, and it looked exactly as it was before. Geoffrey was there smiling and waiting, holding his three-year-old son, Enoch, in his arms. This not only made him easy for Toni and I to spot, but also calmed our spirits. Despite being the clear minorities in the room, it suddenly felt like family picking us up from the airport.

Our car ride was long and bumpy, but pleasant. It was late at night, so there was nothing to see but darkness and stars as we drove. Little Enoch fell asleep with his head on my lap, which I loved. It was a nice reminder for me that we were there to offer our support, and help make a difference for children just like him. It was close to midnight when we got to our motel, so after Geoffrey helped us secure our rooms, they departed and would be back for us in the morning to visit the school. (As much as I would love to continue talking about this trip in detail, I have to remind myself – this is one short story about the school project. Perhaps the next book I write will be entitled *It's Africa To Me*, so forgive me as I try to stay on topic.)

The school was just as Geoffrey said it was and the children were so grateful and excited for the building to be finished. Initially, they were timid, most had never seen a *Mzungu* in person before. (Mzungu is a Swahili word used throughout Uganda referring to non-African people, meaning "white-skinned.") When these African children looked into our eyes, and reached out to touch us while whispering *Mzungu*, we felt like angels. We tried not to let these children's pure hearts and excitement cloud our judgment in our quest to seek our continued role in this project.

But even with all the joy and excitement, there were aspects that were confusing to us as well. It was hard for us to distinguish what was merely a cultural difference and what was not quite right. We had been told we would meet the Board of Directors that were advising and securing additional funds for this project. But we never did, and were simply told that they were not able to travel to come. I do believe they exist, I just don't think their role was as active as implied. As much as we had asked Geoffrey to not elevate us, he did. In fact, while we were visiting, Uganda was preparing for the Pope, who would be driving through their countryside in the next month. There were signs, banners, and decorations to celebrate his arrival. Within only a few days of being there, we began to wonder if we were the Pope. The hype that Geoffrey had built up in others toward us was evident. Toni and I felt these beautiful people of God were now relying more on us for their future than the Lord. As much as we wanted to believe we were helping, we understood more and more each day that while our generosity did buy land and build a foundation for this school, it had also broadened their dreams and taken the focus off who the True Builder of this school was. Geoffrey had plaques made in our honor, and held a ceremony honoring us with hundreds of people in attendance. He spoke of their many friends in America and the future plans that would take continued funding - money he indirectly expected us and *our friends* to raise and then entrust to him. In that moment, I realized that I should have gone through an established organization like African Renewal Ministries, who I had come out with on my first trip to Uganda. It's just not as simple as giving a trustworthy person money and watching lives change. I was not upset with Geoffrey. He was a good man and was doing the best he could with what knowledge he had. But, like me, he is a gifted teacher with a big heart, not a project manager. I was, however, upset with myself. I dangled the hope of a miracle in front of a man with God-sized dreams. Do I continue trying to raise funds out of a sense of obligation, or do I do what I set out to do from the start: trust God apart from myself?

Currently being in a position of complete reliance on Geoffrey for our safety, care, and travel, Toni and I agreed not to discuss our hesitations about moving forward with this project with Geoffrey until after we returned home. Our email exchanges in the weeks and months to come were not easy but confirmed Geoffrey's desperate reliance on us and us alone. It was more than just putting a roof on what we started. There would always be more to do and more to fund. Finding supporters and sponsors to sustain this school would easily become a full-time job for both of us. We wanted more than anything to see this school completed as we worked with Geoffrey in this shared goal. But somewhere in our language barrier, we went from giving some support, to being the

support. It was not ours to complete and while we physically walked away, we never gave up hope, remembering **Phillippians 1:6**: being confident of this, that He who began a good work in you will carry it on to completion until the day of Christ Jesus.

Our prayer that day at Starbucks was that the money we were sending would arrive there safely and be used to purchase land and begin building a school where poor African children could learn and grow. And just like the stranger at the bank said, God did answer that prayer. But like King David, it was not ours to finish, and like the expectations of the exiled people of Babylon, it may not be completed as originally planned.

A few years later, God proved faithful to His promise. It may not have happened in our way or in our timing, as there were lessons that first needed to be learned from both sides of the globe. But God's Glory School was eventually roofed and continues to grow!

Then the people of Israel – the priests, the Levites and the rest of the exiles – celebrated the dedication of the house of God with joy.

Update:

Here is an email I received from Geoffrey the week of Christmas 2020:

Hello Kim,

I hope this email finds you well.

I would like to wish you Merry Christmas and prosperous New Year 2021.

I will forever be grateful to God for bringing you into my life. Your life has continued to impact my life. Your persistence in praying and seeking God amidst storms can't go unmentioned.

May God bless you and increase you.

Blessings
Geoffrey

A NEW PERSPECTIVE

Nehemiah is an Israelite official who strives to build a wall around
Jerusalem and is met with opposition from the surrounding people.
The prophet Zechariah had preached that God intended the new city
to be without walls, welcoming people from all nations to come and
join God's people. Nehemiah had his own ideas to what God intended.
Both the Israelites and Nehemiah are in need of some **spiritual renewal
and new hearts that are open to obedience.**

....

"Do you need a spanking?"

Have you ever heard a parent ask this ridiculous question? Despite your
opinion on the controversial subject, I think we can all agree that no
child will respond, "Oh, yes please, that's just what I need."

What is the purpose of a spanking? Perhaps it's to provide a consequence for wrong behavior, or to serve as a tool in training little ones
to be safe and respectful by remembering the sting of disobedience.
Whatever the reason for giving a spanking, the desired result is usually
the same: to gain a new perspective.

I had a friend from church, who actually coined this phrase when
disciplining her daughter. Instead of asking if she needed a spanking,
she would simply turn to her during times of extreme conflict and ask,
"Do you need a new perspective?" Her daughter, even at a very young
age, knew exactly what her mother meant. She either needed to change
her behavior or a swat to her backside was imminent. Clearly, gaining
a new perspective on the situation would be in her best interest. And
because her mother was characterized by following through with
her words, this little girl often changed her ways before a "new
perspective" was ever given.

This also proved to be a valuable tool in public places. Let's face it: Nobody in line next to you at the grocery store is going to give you a dirty look for asking your child if she needs a new perspective. In fact, the little girl's quick change in behavior after hearing these big words was often inspiring to bystanders.

It is easy for me to look back on times when I clearly needed a new perspective on the situation. One might even say I could use a spiritual spanking from the Lord to humble myself. I find this particularly true when dealing with my own children. Just because we're the adults doesn't mean we know everything. I have learned time and time again to stop and listen to these little ones before anger and pride take over. Let me share two of these humbling experiences with you.

When Blake was three years old, he began coloring pictures at Sunday School to proudly bring home. Those of you who have experienced your child handing you their first work of art, done outside of your presence, know what a special moment this can be. Well, my moment was tainted by a black crayon. You see, my son would color me a picture using nothing but a black crayon week after week.

I asked him if there were other colors available at Sunday School. "Yes, lots. But I like this one the best." His teachers on Sunday mornings assured me that they would offer him other colors, but he always replied, "no thank you." Having a Bachelor's Degree in Child Development with a Minor in Psychology, I was concerned that this was a clear textbook sign of being depressed and disturbed.

Somehow, ignoring the problem didn't make it go away. So finally, after three Sundays of black artwork on my fridge, I sat Blake down at the kitchen table and invited him to color. Sure enough, he quickly found the black crayon and before it even touched the paper, I asked the long overdue question, "Why that one?"

Blake simply pointed to the writing on the neatly wrapped dark stick of wax and said,

"Look Mommy, it's almost my name." (SMACK - insert spiritual spanking here)

Above his sweet chubby finger, I saw the small letters b-l-a-c-k. I had never made the connection to how close those letters were to b-l-a-k-e. My little boy went from being mentally disturbed to mentally gifted in a matter of seconds. All I had to do was ask.

God must have known that as humans, He would need to remind us to be slow to anger and quick to listen. I remember reading this in the Bible, and as I turned to my Concordance to reference which verse it was, I found it in at least seven different places. This reminded me, as a parent, when we really want our kids to know something, we will repeat it again and again. God clearly wants us to know this.

Do you know how many situations could have been better in your life if you had just listened? Well, God does. And as a loving parent, He's going to remind us again and again. He doesn't want life to be difficult or painful. He has equipped us with so many "secrets for success" in His Word. Let's be quick to listen to them.

About a year after the crayon lesson, I was picking up my (almost two-year-old) Ryan, from his Sunday School class. As I walked through the door, I saw all the painted projects on the table, ready to be taken home. I picked up Ryan's all-blue paper and lifted my eyes to see my son with a matching blue-painted face. The paint was all over his lips and cheeks. My first assumption: These teachers were not doing their job and neglected to watch my little guy as he tried to eat the (hopefully non-toxic) paint.

Finding myself on the church grounds again and remembering my last slow-to-listen experience, I took a deep breath as the lady with the paint-stained apron came rushing towards me.

"I am so sorry, Ryan's Mom, I couldn't catch him in time."

Breathe, breathe, keep listening, bite your tongue, don't say what you're thinking.

"Today we learned how Jesus healed the sick," she said. "After Ryan painted, he bent down to kiss the picture of the sick little girl on the paper. I saw it coming and I just couldn't stop him in time. I wiped his face right away and although safe, I made sure that none of the paint got in his mouth."

I smiled at her, as if I knew there had to be a reasonable explanation. It was clear this woman felt terrible despite the fact that she did everything right. How grateful I was that I hadn't spewed my anger all over the room. I seized the familiar smack of humbleness in that moment and told this loving volunteer, " Thank you, your Bible lesson clearly reached more than my child's face today."

If I had known back in 2001 that my Black Crayon Scribbler was going to one day get a scholarship to a private college and then graduate after only three years, I wouldn't have cared what his coloring looked like. Nor would I have cared, if my blue-faced baby kissed every painted page of the sick little girl, considering the generous and compassionate man he is now demonstrating to be. The truth is, we have no idea how God is working behind the scenes to accomplish future greatness in our kids.

It's easy to grow weary with the "I don't understands" or the inconveniences of this world. But the Lord has a plan. So go to Him and ask for that humble spirit (an ability to listen when you want to scream). Ask for Him to give you a new perspective on a grim situation. But be prepared. Sometimes the sting of a spiritual spanking is not what we want, but is just what we need.

Nehemiah 9:17
They refused to listen and failed to remember the miracles you performed among them. ... But you are a forgiving God, gracious and compassionate, slow to anger and abounding in love. Therefore you did not desert them.

FOR SUCH A TIME AS THIS

I recently learned that Esther is the only book of the Bible that never mentions God by name. While God's work is clearly shown throughout, the name of God is never actually uttered. In fact, Esther is given explicit instructions at the beginning of her journey not to tell anyone that she is a Jew. Instead, her character and gentle spirit speak louder than any pre-judged label could.

....

While my Christian faith may stem back to my early childhood years, I am by no means always comfortable talking about it. In my heart, I have the deepest desire for everyone to know the Lord. Not only for the obvious eternal-life-benefit, but also because I know the peace and hope He brings in this earthly life. Nevertheless, when it comes to the gift of evangelizing, I don't have it. I freeze up. I chicken out. I don't want to be rejected and appear to push my personal belief on others. Yet, as a child of God, greatly impacted by the saving grace of Jesus, shouldn't I naturally want to be shouting it out for all to hear?

So, this became my prayer: Lord, bring me opportunities where I can comfortably yet boldly share You with others. (I know, I know... You don't call us to be comfortable.) But I believe You've gifted me in being a diligent peacemaker, and it's near impossible to keep the peace while creating awkward moments as I impart my faith to others. But YOU are God and I am not, so I trust <u>You</u> will somehow use me, in light of how You've created me.

Within days of this prayer, I found myself in a situation I was sure God wanted me to suit up for the frontlines. On Thursday mornings, a few of us moms go for a hike after dropping our kids off at middle school. This one particular Thursday morning, our friend Pam brought her neighbor, Beth. Pam mentioned to me privately that her neighbor was an atheist. "This was it!" I thought. "I'm ready, God! Use me!"

Beth was friendly, but very quiet. She didn't talk much about her own life and was clearly there for the fresh air and exercise. Every Thursday I would pray and ask God to please help me find a way to work Jesus as Savior into our conversations. But each week we all just talked about our family struggles, our upcoming weekends, kids going through puberty, teachers' high expectations, and life as we each personally navigate through it.

After about six weeks of Thursday hikes, Beth's work schedule changed and she could no longer join us. I was so disappointed in myself. All that time and I never once talked about Jesus and His love and sacrifice for us all! What kind of Christian am I? In my heart, I felt I had let God down. He gave me an opportunity and I blew it.

A few weeks later, I was chatting with Pam and she asked, "Did I ever tell you what my neighbor, Beth, said about you?"

"Uh... no," was my baffled response.

Pam continued, "Beth said that you were the best example of a Christian she had ever seen."

"What?! Why?!" I questioned. "I've been beating myself up for not being more bold with her and putting myself out there to talk about Jesus," I admitted.

"Well, she said, she really appreciated how you didn't try and

jam Christianity down her throat. She liked how you would just talk about your life, and how you try and raise your kids well, and how you clearly have a heart for others," Pam relayed.

I told Pam, I didn't even remember telling Beth I was a Christian. Pam then reminded me that I talked about my kids going to youth camp with our church, and how I'd shared some of my Africa experiences while we hiked, and how I mentioned prayer and overcoming some tough times through God's grace.

"You did tell her you were a Christian, you just didn't realize it," Pam explained. "Beth simply needed someone to make faith in God look attractive, and you did that."

Wow! God did use me! It may not have resulted in a tearful confession of sins and a "drop to your knees and surrender your life over to Jesus kind of moment," but I'm okay with that. Beth didn't need another person showing her the light via high beam. In that moment, she needed an example of someone experiencing the joy of the Lord in a subtle glow, so she could look directly into the light. I've learned that I'm more of a seed planter than a harvester and God created me that way for such a time as this.

Esther 4:14

For if you remain silent at this time, relief and deliverance for the Jews will arise from another place, but you and your father's family will perish. And who knows but you have come to your royal position for such a time as this.

HE'S GOT A CHAPTER 42 FOR YOU

Even if you have never read the Bible, you probably know the story of Job. Satan makes a statement to God that the only reason Job worships the Lord is because he is so richly blessed. **Job is a righteous and blameless man** with a true and pure heart for the Lord. Job loses his children, his livestock, his health, and all of his wealth because **God allows Satan to test him**. It addresses the timeless question: Why would God allow good people to suffer?

When I look back at the first 40 years of my life, I realize now how easy, carefree and protected it was. I grew up in a home with two loving parents who remained married "til death-did-them-part," a younger sister who was my built-in playmate, and a big back yard that made it easy to ignore the unpredictable world outside its gates. In fact, my dad laid a concrete path around the perimeter of our large property so that his two little girls could ride their bikes freely within the safety of its boundaries. My dad also built us a two-story playhouse and dug a 6-foot deep swimming pool, while we played house and rode our bikes with bells that dinged around him.

My mom worked for the airlines, so between our family flying for free and constantly finding deals and discounts on travel, we vacationed a lot. I went to private Christian schools from nursery on up to high school. I had lots of friends, rarely got picked last for kickball, and usually got a part in the school play. My teachers were kind to me and my parents were perfectly content with my B's and C's. I went to college close to home, became a teacher, and married my high school sweetheart. We lived near my parents in a townhome that they gifted to me after graduating college. I never knew what it was like to pay off student loans, make rent for an apartment, or have to look for a babysitter once our children were born. My husband and I were well respected in the community as a soccer coach and a school teacher. We went to church on Sundays, attended mid-week Bible studies, and even facilitated a parenting class.

Now, before you roll your eyes and slam this book shut, I'm not saying my life was without any hardships. I've shared in other stories that my mom was diagnosed with a debilitating disease when I was a teenager and my marriage had its struggles years before our divorce. But for the most part, like Job, I was richly blessed by God and felt His love for me everyday… Then I hit 40!

Becoming pregnant at age 40 was not my plan, but the idea of God bringing us a baby to strengthen our weakening family dynamic made me quickly warm up to the idea. In the three months that I was pregnant, I planned out God's perfect path for our family's future, only to have that plan destroyed in the blink of an eye. It was my start to what it must feel like to be "sifted by Satan." After a devastating miscarriage, my marriage only got worse, leading to separation and then divorce. I moved from a 3,200-square-foot home in the coveted hills of Porter Ranch, to a 200-square foot home in my parents' backyard. I went from caring for my children everyday, to legally not being able to see them on

Mondays, Tuesdays, and every other weekend. Our family of four that once shared things openly, now seemed to be defined by secrets to protect the boys, while they too were cautious to protect each parent's feelings. I also perceived my own parents' disappointment each day I went up to the main house. I tried to go back to teaching, but it broke my heart to involve myself so closely to children and parents whose families were intact and who were actively enjoying the very thing that was ripped from me.

Then out of nowhere, my dad died suddenly and my mom was left without the love of her life and her full-time caregiver. I took over, but Satan liked to whisper in my ear, "You're a 45-year-old woman with a college degree and you basically lift your mom onto the toilet for a living." One son moved to Texas and shortly after the other son moved away with his dad full-time. I tried to date, but it was disastrous because I was constantly in healing mode and overly sensitive to getting or giving rejection. Therapy helped, but sadly I couldn't turn that office couch into my bed. Eventually, I had to walk out and face all the harsh realities I had just come to terms with. There were a few rare moments when I wanted to heed Job's wife's advice and just "curse God and die." But despite everything I just listed, I knew, "God's got me." In fact, I felt God's presence daily, more during this time of my life than I did in my first 40 years.

There is a poem I clung to by Mary Stevenson entitled Footprints in the Sand. The speaker walks with the Lord down the beach and questions why during the most difficult times of her life, she was left alone as there are no longer two sets of footprints visible in the sand. The poem ends with this line:

> He whispered, "My precious child, I love you and will
> never leave you

Never, ever, during your trials and testings.

When you saw only one set of footprints,

It was then that I carried you."

True, while I sometimes grew discouraged and questioned God, I knew that I could trust Him to carry me through. Perhaps one day I will look back and see why these hardships made sense to God. But for now, I'm looking forward to my Chapter 42.

Job 42:12
The Lord blessed the latter part of Job's life more than the first.

Whether my Chapter 42 is to come in this life or the next, that's not for me to know right now. But I do know that as believers, we are all promised a Chapter 42 in our books. This year during a global pandemic, many people may feel like Job as they are in the "how long must I suffer" part of their book. But here's what I think. We as a world are being forced to stop and evaluate our lives, to realize our powerlessness, and to be honest about our relationships and life choices. In the past, we've been able to push aside our problems or avoid looking at the long term because we are too busy in the now. Today, you can't use television or social media as a distraction because it's filled with reminders, warnings, and statistics that require you to take action. You can't take off to the movies, or a bar, or your workplace to escape reality anymore. We are forced to stay home and live with ourselves. Like Job, your health, your family, your finances, and your future may be at risk. And hopefully, like Job, you are turning to God in a way you never have before and trusting Him when nothing makes sense – yet.

Job 42:5
My ears had heard of you but now my eyes have seen you.

FEARFULLY AND WONDERFULLY MADE

Psalms is a collection of 150 poems, songs and prayers of both lament and praise to our Lord, written by the prophet David and a handful of others, some anonymous. Each psalm is personal to the author but there is a general theme to **not ignore the pains of this life**, and instead, express them and then anticipate a future without pain with **hopefulness and a deeper understanding of God's love**. The letter you will read below is my own expression of lament and praise. I wrote it 12 hours after my miscarriage and only intended it to be between me and its recipient, but God works in mysterious ways.

....

Dear Baby,

I'm writing you a letter you will never read. As difficult as this is, the need for me to express my love for you far exceeds the need to push this pain away. It all happened so fast, I'm still trying to wrap my mind around it.

January 13, 2012, 5:00 p.m. I got up from resting to use the bathroom. I had been having some slight stomach cramps throughout the day, so I thought I'd lay down for a bit. While peeing, I felt something pass through me. It wasn't painful, but I knew it wasn't right. "Please God, NO," I remember saying as I reached for the bathroom light. I turned to see two drops of blood on the floor and my heart fell. Realizing that gravity was not my friend right now; my first instinct was to lay on my bed.

Your daddy and oldest brother, Blake, were at a soccer practice. Thankfully, your 12-year-old brother, Ryan, was in his room and came running as soon as I called his name. "Ry, something's wrong. I need you to grab my cell phone so that I can call the doctor."

Now 5:08pm, the doctor was gone, but the answering service assured me she would call me back. I hung up and asked Ryan if he would please pray, for I could not. "Dear, Lord…" then the phone rang. Dr. Silberstein assured me that cramping and spotting were normal in the first trimester (even though I was in my second). As for the feeling of something passing through me – that she could not explain. When I got off the phone, I knew I would have to investigate. Ryan got me a towel, as I returned to the bathroom. I told him, I had no idea what I was about to pull out of there and if he wanted to leave I would completely understand.

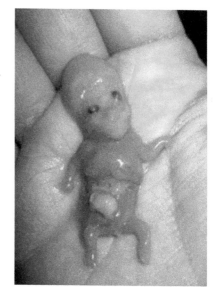

"I'm staying," came his unwavering answer.

I reached to the back of the toilet with strength that was not my own. The next thing I remember is opening my hand to see you for the first time; a perfect, intact 13-week-old fetus. I was shocked.

"That's our baby," Ryan blurted.

We stood there just staring at you in disbelief. Your eyes were the bluest eyes I'd ever seen. There were your legs and arms, I could even count your fingers and toes. And from what I could tell, the boys would have gotten their wish for another brother. You seemed to have all that you needed. Why are you here so soon? Too soon!

I pushed re-dial on the phone and told my doctor what I held in my hand. She of course was so sorry for my loss, but so surprised at the way it happened. Most miscarriages are not that clean and few ever allow you to hold your baby - well at least not at 13 weeks.

I got off the phone and all I could think was, "How do I put you back? I have to put you back!" I mustered the strength to tell Ryan that for some reason this baby was needed more in Heaven than on Earth. I felt like I had to say something to make it okay. Most of the time, your brother Ryan has a maturity beyond his years that I find a little scary, but on days like today, it clearly is a gift and a blessing. He calmly looked into my eyes and said, "Things happen for a reason," and with that he hugged me - I mean he really hugged me.

We put you in a small glass bowl with some water so that Daddy and Blake could see you and say goodbye to you. Ryan went off to his room for some alone time. Unable to get ahold of your dad earlier, he called me back to see what was up. Your conception was a bit of a surprise, but your untimely birth was a shock neither of us were prepared for. He kept saying, "I am so sorry." After 18 years of marriage, I knew he meant he was sorry for all of us. For the last three months, the four of us grew more and more excited each day. We bonded as a family discussing your development, your gender, and your possible name. We were so excited when we could finally send your ultrasound picture through emails, texts, and social media to let all of our friends and family know of our uncontainable joy. Now, within only seconds, it was taken away from us.

I got off the phone with your dad, and in God's perfect timing, began going through the process of delivering the sack and all that comes with the miracle of birth. (This was the step my doctor couldn't explain me skipping.) But right then I knew... God gave me not only the opportunity to hold my baby, completely intact, without distraction or pain, but he waited on "the yucky stuff." He is a just God, despite my grim situation.

By the time your dad and Blake walked through the door, the reality of it all had set in. Ryan came out of his room and shared our sad news with Blake. The two of them are so different. Blake is so much like your dad, not quite sure how to give in to his emotions, needing extra time to walk away and process things. This worked out well, for Ryan and I had shared all the words we needed. Now we all just shared understanding looks of heartbreak and the comfort that can only come from the hug of someone who is feeling your same pain.

They saw you, were amazed by you, and then couldn't look anymore. Ryan and I kept coming back to you, learning something new that we hadn't seen before, etching you into our memory. But we all deal with grief differently and that's perfectly okay.

I took this photo of you. It seemed strange to want to capture the moment. But I somehow had such a feeling of peace and I knew God was going to reveal things to me over time. Anyway, I didn't find you gross and unfinished. Honestly, you were one of the most precious things I had ever seen. Seeing you made it real to me, to us, and I knew there were lots of others out there who had also fallen in love with the idea of you. It might help them to say goodbye as well.

Before I let you go, I want to tell you that your life was not a waste. I am certain there are moments to come, lives that will be touched, and miracles we may never know about. I am proud to be your mom and honored to have been able to hold you for a brief moment here on Earth. I will always remember January 13, as the day you came into the world and changed my life forever. This will not be known as the date that I lost you, rather, the date that I glimpsed at eternity and felt the hand of God upon me.

So goodbye my sweet baby, but just for a while. I know with great certainty that I will see you again. And I know until that day – you will be in the best of hands.

I love you,
Mommy

Psalms 139:14

I praise you for I am fearfully and wonderfully made; your works are wonderful, I know that full well

IRON SHARPENS IRON

The word *proverb* refers to a short clever saying that provides wisdom. The Book of Proverbs is full of such sayings that offer **wisdom from God**. Unlike other books of the Bible, these are not laws but rather **God's invitation to learn**. It is also not a book of promises, but a book of probabilities should you adhere to the lessons. Proverbs offers practical skills to living well in this world God created.

....

A brother in Christ, and a fellow Kindergarten parent, was short a player for that night's game in his men's baseball league. I was still married at the time and my husband loved sports and was decently athletic, so he agreed to fill the vacant spot. Later that evening, upon returning home from the game, he announced, "That John is an amazing man!"

"Oh, he's a good baseball player?" I asked.

"Yes, but he's an even better Christian," he replied. "He has so much passion and boldness for the Lord. I wish I could step out in faith like that!" My husband did not grow up going to church or experiencing a relationship with the Lord, but he always admired this quality in other men. It wasn't until we were dating that he really opened his heart and mind to faith in Jesus. He admired many of the men he would meet at church and wanted their conviction to be able to speak with such godly confidence. But to him it felt forced, unnatural and awkward. He never really understood that confidence in the Lord is not a persona that you strive for - it comes naturally after developing a personal relationship with God over time. **It's easier to bring God out in public when you spend quality time with Him in private**. That always seemed to be the piece that was missing for him, the piece our friend John had, and that was evident in situations like this.

He proceeded to tell me that this baseball team was through the Department of Parks and Recreation, and apparently John was new to them as well. Based on some of the pre-game "trash talk," it was proving to be quite a competitive group of guys, from all walks of life. Early predictions showed that it was shaping up to be a heated game. So it took my husband (and I'm sure everybody else) by surprise when John announced, "Hey, before we play, let's all take a knee for our troops." Not only did every player on their team take a knee, but the opposing team came over and joined in as well. According to this recount of events, our friend not only confidently prayed for our soldiers on the battlefields of Iraq, but smoothly transitioned into speaking into existence the players positive sportsmanship on the recreational field before them.

The reality of soldiers concurrently sacrificing their lives, while they play ball in the park, was brilliant. Collectively, these two groups of opposing men were voluntarily inviting the Lord to their baseball game. And the game that followed reflected that. I could easily see why my husband felt both inspired and inadequate all at the same time.

Fast forward to the next day when John picked up his son, Max, from outside my classroom. As I saw him walking towards me I announced, "Oh look, here comes the superhero." Max's daddy, of course, humbly looked behind him to see where "the superhero" was. After seeing no one else around, he smiled and asked, "Me a superhero? What are you talking about? You're the one who manages kindergartners all day."

I replayed for him the events as told to me, and what an amazing impact his brave and bold call-to-action not only had on his last-minute teammate, but apparently every guy who came to play ball that night.

John looked me straight in the eye and said, "Oh, that was all your husband's doing."

"Really, how so?" I asked.

"Iron sharpens iron," he said without hesitation.

I'm familiar with the verse from Proverbs he was referring to. It represents two believers impacting each other in such a way that they are stronger and sharper for the Lord. But it didn't seem to fit in this case. I mean, it was John who boldly gathered everyone together. It was John who asked strangers to kneel on the ground and bow their heads to a God that many of them might not know. Additionally, the words to John's prayer were so powerful that the blood flowing to these men's hearts overpowered their testosterone. The game that followed was light and fun. All were made graciously aware of their freedom to play.

So I inquired, "How did iron sharpen iron in this case?"

He replied, "If your husband wasn't there, that prayer would have never been prayed aloud. I didn't really know anyone personally on the team. The only reason I had the courage to ask everyone to bring it in and take a knee is because I knew there was at least one other guy on that field who would kneel with me. Having your husband there and knowing he was a Christian too, sharpened me to go for it. God did the rest. Honestly, I had no idea what I was going to pray or how it would be received. I was actually just as in awe as he was. To God be the Glory."

With tears in my eyes, I smiled and nodded my head in agreement. I couldn't wait to get home and retell this valuable lesson: You don't have to speak boldly in order for God to use you. Sometimes you simply need to just show up.

Proverbs 27:17
As iron sharpens iron,
So a man sharpens the countenance of his friend.

I'M PRO-CHOICE TOO!

The book of Ecclesiastes is another book imparting great wisdom.
The author (possibly King Solomon) takes stock of the world as he
reflects back on his life. He addresses that while **life is a gift from
God**, it is fleeting and seemingly meaningless. Ecclesiastes explores
the many ways that we seek meaning apart from God and encourages
us to welcome life as we experience it rather than as we feel we ought
to. While this life is unpredictable, unstable and eventually erased by
time, there is meaning to be found. Total trust in God allows us the
freedom to embrace the life that we've been given, even if it's not
the life that we've planned.

....

In eighth grade, Blake was assigned to give a persuasive speech in his
middle school English class. He took on the topic of pro-life because at
the time he thought it would be an easy one. You see, he had grown up
in a home where life was always valued, where every pregnant couple
he had ever known had been overjoyed by the gift of life that lie within
them. Not to mention the fact that I, his mom, was 13 weeks pregnant
at the time and our whole family was ecstatic about it.

At this ripe age of 14, he was now challenged with views that differed
from the ones his dad and I had tried to instill. So when he read his
speech to me, I was a bit disappointed to hear how "safe" it sounded.
He gave facts and statistics about fetal development and abortion, but
nothing profound that would cause anyone to re-think their own view.
It was a fast read, an informative speech at best. No one would truly
feel persuaded by a speech that lacked emotion, nor attach themself to
a side that even the speaker was unsure about. He then shared with me
that some of his friends and classmates were very much pro-choice
and that they felt that it was unfair to say that a woman can't choose

what happens to her own body. He said he could see that side as well and he didn't want to offend anyone with his speech.

I will never forget the look on his face when I told him, "Actually, I'm pro-choice too." Looking into his wide eyes, I continued, "I believe a man and a woman have the CHOICE to have sex with one another. God then has the CHOICE of whether or not He wants a life to be created. When a couple finds out that they are pregnant, they are to accept the reality that the CHOICES have already been made." With much contemplation, he took my explanation in. Although this topic seemed to be chosen by him at random, it was not random to God. I gave him the 10-week-old ultrasound picture of our baby-in-the-making and said, "Perhaps you should use this." To no surprise, he fought me on it. "Then I'm going to have to tell my whole class who that baby is and that my mom is pregnant," he said.

I knew he wasn't embarrassed about my pregnancy, he just hated the idea of having more attention on him. After attempting a persuasive speech of my own, which included thought-provoking phrases like, "The photo might help you make the argument that you are hesitant to make," and "No matter what, you're going to be uncomfortable, so you might as well be effective and uncomfortable" - he still was opposed to the idea. In the end, he finally agreed to give it a try when I suggested that passing around a picture might take up some of the 2 to 4 minute time requirement.

We practiced over and over until he felt somewhat confident. I even cropped out my name from the ultrasound picture before printing it out for him. This way, his classmates might just think he Googled it. I told him during that week how proud I was of him for stepping out of his comfort zone and taking on a topic that was highly controversial.

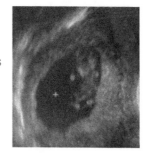

Still clinging onto his fear of public speaking, my son never volunteered himself and finally was one of the last to be chosen at the end of the week. He got in the car after school and said, "It was amazing, one of the best in the class." He even gave the baby's picture credit for his forthcoming A grade. He said that no one else had visuals and that the class was really taken by the photo and were amazed that they could see an actual baby. One boy asked if the ultrasound was of him as a fetus. "No," Blake replied. "It's the baby that is inside my mom right now." Little did we all know that only a few short hours later, I would miscarry and this baby would no longer be. Later, I took some comfort in the thought that perhaps Blake's speech, along with our baby's photo, brought meaning to such a short existence. We never know what impact our current experiences will have on future outcomes. As sad as losing a baby was, in time I had a sense of peace about it. I made the hard CHOICE to trust God and embrace life as I was experiencing it, not as I thought it ought to be.

Ecclesiastes 11:5
As you do not know the path of the wind, or how the body
is formed in a mother's womb, so you cannot understand
the work of God, the Maker of all things.

LULLABY

Solomon's Song of Songs is a collection of love poetry, reflecting on the divine gift of love. While most read this book of the Bible as a passionate love saga between a man and a woman, it also emulates Christ's love for His people. These **"greatest of songs"** celebrate the gift of loving another and point to the ultimate gift of the Father's love.

....

When I was a little girl, for years, my dad would tuck me into bed and sing me Lullaby. I'm not sure of the official lyrics to this song, but here is what I fell asleep to:

> *Lullaby…and goodnight…for your daddy is watching….*
> *Lullaby…go to sleep…for your daddy is here.*
> *Lullaby…and goodnight…for your daddy is watching…*
> *Close your eyes…go to sleep…for your daddy loves you.*

My dad would sing these four lines over and over again until I eventually drifted into a coma-like state and was completely at peace. Most times I would be just conscious enough to sense him leave my side, and tiptoe out the room. I'd smile inwardly at the thought of him proudly believing he successfully got me to sleep.

Many years later, when I too became a parent, I instinctively found myself singing this same song, with modification to one word:

> *Lullaby…and goodnight…for your mommy is watching….*
> *Lullaby… go to sleep…for your mommy is here.*
> *Lullaby …and goodnight…for your mommy is watching…*
> *Close your eyes…go to sleep…for your mommy loves you.*

As I would tiptoe out of my son's room, I truly understood the heart-felt satisfaction my dad must have experienced knowing your child is at peace, and you helped him get there.

On January 18, 2016, my dad collapsed on the bathroom floor during the middle of the night. While my mom lay in her bed, unable to reach the phone on my dad's nightstand, she called out to me. I was asleep in a room at the end of the hallway, but never heard her. Perhaps in a cloudy state of mind, that night my dad closed and locked their bedroom door before going to bed. They never close their door, and I didn't even know it had a lock on it until I tried to open it the next morning. I heard my mom's faint plea from outside the door and called 911 right away. The 911 operator instructed me to break down the door with a running start while pushing my upper arm against it. It broke open immediately and I ran to find my dad, unconscious but still breathing.

Only two weeks before, a small blood clot was detected in his thigh after he had had a minor surgical procedure to relieve the pain from varicose veins. His doctor prescribed a blood thinning medication called Lovenox. My dad felt competent in self-administering the injections twice daily as he had used needles before to give my mom injections for her MS treatments. (He also refused to leave Mom two times a day to drive out to Kaiser, only to wait on a doctor to do what he easily could himself.) It was Day 11 of the 14-day-treatment when he suddenly collapsed.

While I waited for the ambulance, I called my two boys and my sister to please come straight away. My younger son Ryan insisted on staying with his "Mimi," so Blake went with me to the hospital. I stood over my dad's bed in the ER looking at his CT Scan while listening to the doctor explain that the blood clot had traveled to his head and the bleeding was extensive. My dad could possibly survive, he said. But the pressure on his brain was great. It could be released by cracking the skull, but irreparable damage had surely been done, and he would most likely be in a vegetative state for the remainder of his life.

I couldn't understand how this could be happening to the healthiest 83-year-old anyone had ever seen. I began thinking out loud, "Could I have stopped this? What if I had gotten to him at 2 a.m. instead of 7 a.m.? What if the door…"

"Stop, Mom, don't go there," Blake's words interrupted. "This is not your fault, you've done everything you could possibly do for Papa."

How blessed I am that the Lord put my two sons by my side to speak truth over me during such tragic moments! God used Ryan to comfort me a few years before this, as I held his baby brother in my cupped hand. And now He's using Blake to extinguish the flaming arrows of guilt and blame as I hold his Papa's limp hand in my own.

Per his Advanced Directive, it was my dad's wish to not resuscitate or extend life beyond what his body could naturally handle. So the decision not to intervene and to allow his body to shut down and drift from this life to the next was already made years ago, by him. I stood over my dad, kissing his forehead as he lay in the hospital bed. As devastating as it was, he looked so peaceful. He looked just like he did whenever he would fall asleep watching television in his chair: his head cocked to one side, mouth open, and quiet, audible breathing. What happened next, I was not prepared for. The song - our song, the lullaby began to chime from inside the hospital room. I literally shook my head in disbelief, for surely I was delusional and the sound was just in my imagination. My sister, who was standing on the other side of the bed, looked at me with wide, tearful eyes. I knew she heard it too. I glanced back at my dad, who was sleeping so peacefully. I began to mentally place the words to the lullaby in accordance to the chimes. Except this time, the song was being sung to him. Not by me, but by his Heavenly Father…

"Lullaby...and goodnight...for your Father is watching....
Lullaby...go to sleep...for your Savior is here.
Lullaby ...and goodnight...for your Father is watching...
Close your eyes...go to sleep...for your Daddy loves you."

A moment later, a nurse walked in and casually asked, "Did you hear the lullaby chimes?" I just stared back at her; a loss for words. She smiled and continued, "Lullaby chimes play throughout the whole hospital each time a baby is born in our delivery room."

God's timing is rarely our timing, but it is inevitably perfect timing.

In that moment, I could feel my Father's arms around me as I placed mine around my dad. It was then that I understood my strong immortal daddy would not be coming back to us. Another harsh reality in my life, and once again God shows me that He is right there holding me.

Exactly one week later, my dad finished sleeping ...and woke-up to see the face of the One who is always watching, is always here, and always loves you.

Song of Songs 2:10-12
My beloved spoke and said to me, "Arise, my darling, my beautiful one, come with me. See! The winter is past; the rains are over and gone. Flowers appear on the Earth; the season of singing has come, the cooing of doves is heard in our land.

CLOUDS OF HOPE

The Book of Isaiah proclaims both judgment and hope. A judgment that states rebellion against God will come at a cost, and a hope that God's covenant promises will be fulfilled. Isaiah prophesizes of a Servant who will come and of a new Heaven and a new Earth that will be inherited. The New Testament often refers back to the prophesies of Isaiah, both fulfilled and yet to be fulfilled.

As children of God, we need not fear the pain and adversities of this world; He has shown us He is faithful to keep His promises.

It was a Friday after school in spring, as I stood in my Kindergarten classroom finishing up a rainbow bulletin board. My students had left for the day, but I stayed to put up their freshly dried artwork. I could just envision their smiling faces come Monday morning as they walked in the classroom and were greeted by their beautiful accomplishments. As I hung up the last tissue papered rainbow, I couldn't help but notice that my bulletin board still looked a little sparse and could use something else. Anxious to start my weekend, I left the large blue space of the board as is. I figured something would come to mind between now and Monday.

My relaxing, lighthearted weekend took a shocking turn after a phone call I received from my friend Christy on Saturday. The father of Landon (one of my Kindergarten students) had passed away late Friday night from a sudden heart attack. Wow! All I could picture was his wife Natasha, devastated and left to care for their 5-and 3-year-old sons. What a tragedy!

The next morning after church, Christy asked if I would go with her to visit Natasha. Without giving it thought, I agreed. We arrived at her home and were greeted at the door by her in-laws, who I sadly realized now outlived their son. I felt like I shouldn't have been there. I am typically a person who finds it natural to comfort others, but I can't begin to imagine what it would be like to lose a husband or an adult child. Why did I come? We entered the kitchen, where I saw Natasha hunched over the center island. Thankfully, Landon and his little brother were at a friend's house. For me, having two sons of similar ages would make seeing her little boys more than I could bear. I had no words of comfort or wisdom for this family in such deep pain. I found it difficult to even make eye contact with any of them throughout my brief visit. I can recall Christy faithfully leading us in prayer as we all held hands in a circle. I so admired her words of hope and godly encouragement during this time of devastation. God put it on her heart to visit and then clearly gave her the right words to say. We were all touched by her Spirit–filled prayer and the awkwardness of being there was gone. Our visit was brief and my words were few. But I realized then, that the Lord had put this visit on Christy's heart and then equipped her for the moment. My role was to be a supportive friend, and that I did. As Natasha walked us to the door she quietly informed me that Landon would be at school tomorrow. She wanted as much normalcy as possible for him. She felt that being with his friends and keeping busy was the best thing for him. I couldn't have agreed more.

Later that evening as I was laying in bed, I began to grow anxious of what lay ahead for me in the morning. Would Landon just break out in tears in the middle of class? Would I be strong enough to keep my own emotions in check? Would questions be asked of me that I had no answers for? I rolled over to see my sleeping husband and closed my eyes listening to him breathe. I then pictured Blake and Ryan peacefully asleep in their rooms knowing all was right in their world. I was so grateful for what I had, and so broken for what Natasha had lost.

The morning came quickly and I was soon busied by the rush of getting us all out the door. It wasn't until I was sitting in my classroom, taking roll that I remembered my fear of this day. Landon was absent; I guess God knew I couldn't handle it. About 20 minutes into our morning the door of my Kindergarten classroom opened. In walked Landon who hurried to his cubby to put his things away. Natasha was behind him wearing large dark sunglasses and carrying a visible burden that no young mother should ever have to bear. As she found her way to my desk, she whispered, "It's been a really rough morning, please don't mention his dad at all today." I bit my lip to hold back tears of my own, and nodded. She gave her son a hug and quickly left.
Although sad, I was also a little relieved. She had made it clear: Don't go there. So I was off the hook; I'll just go about the day as if it were the same as any other.

I announced to the class that it was time to all go sit on the rug for "Calendar and Story." Once we were all seated, one of my young students raised his hand.

"Landon's dad died on Friday," he said.

The half of the class that already knew stared at me for a reaction. The rest of the children stared at Landon in disbelief, and Landon stared down at his lap.

For a split second I panicked. His mom had just given me explicit instructions to avoid this very topic. I felt like I was in one of those commercials, "Need to get away?" But instead of running, I thought, "Need to get God!" I inwardly asked for His help.

Then an unbelievable feeling came over me. A smile stretched across my face that I couldn't control. I stared straight back into those frightened little faces and confidently said, "I know! And do you know where his daddy is right now? He's in Heaven with Jesus! I know his daddy believed in Jesus because he taught Landon about what it means to know Jesus." (Just a few weeks prior Landon had shared with the class about the time his dad prayed with him as Landon asked Jesus into his heart). I continued to talk about the joys of Heaven and soon my smile proved to be contagious. It was as if Jesus himself walked into my classroom and said, "Kim, you sit over here, I got this one."

The words that came out of my mouth were not premeditated. And looking back, I don't even think they were my own. I don't remember all that I said, but what I won't ever forget were the 24 sets of hope-filled eyes looking up at me as I spoke. Then I (or maybe it was the Holy Spirit) asked the students if any of them knew of someone who was in Heaven with Landon's daddy? Hands shot up: my Grandma Rose, my Uncle George, my next-door neighbor, my dog (it's fine, I wasn't tackling that one today). While they shared, I walked to the cupboard in search of white construction paper. Grabbing the scissors, I quickly cut stacks of paper into cloud shapes. As a child would call out a Heavenly name, I would hand him/her a cloud and say, "Go get a marker and write that name on this cloud." Being they were only five, I helped with spelling and offered some suggestions to those students who had never known someone personally who had gone to Heaven. "Think of a person from the Bible or from history, who you believe knew Jesus before they died." So Mary, Zacchaeus and Abraham Lincoln each had a cloud with their name on it.

When Landon handed me his cloud that read "Dad" on it, he asked if he could have another one. On the second cloud he wrote his uncle's name. I later learned that his dad's younger brother had died a few years back in a motorcycle accident. I believe knowing that the two were together in Heaven gave Landon some comfort. I collected 28 clouds and stuck them on the rainbow bulletin board. It was no longer "missing something." I then added these words to the top of the bulletin board in big bold lettering: God Always Keeps His Promises. I watched as the students (Landon included) stared at the board in awe, contemplating that all those people were together with Jesus right now. It was a moment I will never forget.

As we walked out the door for recess I recall thinking, "What just happened in there?" I remembered that Natasha had asked me not to talk about the very thing I just dedicated an hour and 20 minutes to. But the truth is: I didn't go there - God did. He orchestrated it all; I merely walked down the path He had showed me.

Isaiah 41:13

For I am the Lord, your God, who takes hold of your right hand and says to you, Do not fear; I will help you.

JEREMIAH'S JOURNEY

Jeremiah is a prophet who was called to warn Israel about the severe consequences of breaking their covenant with God through idolatry and injustice. His message is to **bring about both justice and grace** as he denounces their behavior and **shares a little glimmer of hope** that will lead to a better future.

....

It wasn't until months after my miscarriage that I named my baby Jeremiah. "Logan" had been the initial name we had picked out. But after holding him in the palm of my hand, as if I was holding a piece of Heaven here on Earth; I knew he needed a different name. To me, Logan is a little boy that plays in the mud, or builds a fort in the living room with his big brothers. That's the baby I thought I was getting, but it's not the baby I had. While still attempting to heal from my loss, I sought out a Bible verse that I vaguely remembered:

Jeremiah 1:5
Before I formed you in the womb I knew you, before you were born I set you apart.

This verse never meant much to me before, but now it means everything. For if God knew the prophet Jeremiah this way, God knows all of us this way. So not only did God know my baby before he was created in my womb, but He had set him apart for some specific purpose. It was hard for me to think back on my baby's tiny and lifeless disposition, and believe that God had a plan for him. But I do recall, as I scooped him up and looked into his captivating blue eyes, that I somehow felt his journey was not over. With God, nothing is wasted, and in my core I knew He would use this little life for more than just something that would inspire awe in me. I named him Jeremiah so that I would always be reminded of God's words over Jeremiah the prophet, and God's words to me. This verse also proved to me that God's definition of a viable life is very different from man's definition. Oh the joy I felt realizing that not only must Baby Jeremiah be experiencing Heaven with Jesus, but so were the two other babies I had miscarried years before - both at even earlier stages of pregnancy. It was after this realization that I decided to start a blog and enclose my Dear Baby letter and Jeremiah's photo, so that other hurting parents could know with certainty that their babies were in Heaven with Jesus too.

At the end of 2012, I received an email from Wordpress.com with my blog's site stats for the year. I was getting nearly 100 views a day on the "Dear Baby" blog post. I then looked over at the list of search engines and saw that "Google Images" was the primary source leading people to my blog. Sure enough, when I Googled 13-week-fetus, little Jeremiah's photo (in the palm of my hand) was among the images that popped up. I then learned that since my blog is open to the public, so are the images that appear on it. At first I found this horrifying. "How do I get him off of this? I don't want strangers gawking at his picture without knowing my heart and his story! How will people react to such an image without my letter of love that accompanies it?!" I then compared him to the other images on the page. I have to admit; he did stand out. The others were mostly small plastic replicas, or sonograms from inside the womb, or even in pieces from what I assume to be photos taken after abortions. Jeremiah's image was very different. When I clicked on his image, it enlarged and I could see a link at the bottom leading viewers to my blog. I continued clicking, as I hoped others would do. When I got to my blog, I noticed there had been comments left at the end of my Dear Baby letter; many from friends. But this one stood out, from a name I did not know:

This baby bridges the gap between Pro Life and Pro Choice.
This photo is not about politics or religion or even one's personal
beliefs - it's just a fact. Evidence of life from the start, for all the
world to see.

Amen. Remembering that God has always been in charge of this amazing life, I let go of my need to control the process. The name Jeremiah means "one who uplifts." Who am I to stand in his way? I forced myself to practice what I preached: "God is bigger than any giant we may face," even a giant named the World Wide Web. And I soon learned just how much bigger He truly was. As of today, my blog has over 40,000 views in nearly 100 different countries.

Jeremiah 1:5 goes on to say, I have appointed you a prophet to the nations. When I first looked up this verse, I skimmed over this second half. I felt that these additional words to the prophet Jeremiah did not apply to my situation. This reminded me that all of the Bible is God breathed and we don't get to pick and choose which parts we want to apply to our lives. God wants us to consider every word. So as further stated in Jeremiah 1:5, this baby has gone global and is literally speaking to nations. The desire to know the truth about the unborn is universal. Looking at the shaded regions on the map to the left - and visualizing the places this baby has gone - gives me chills. Spreading the knowledge that life is fearfully and wonderfully made in every stage of the process. As his mom, I couldn't be more proud. Hearts all over the world are being awakened by Baby Jeremiah. He continues to touch more lives at 13 weeks gestation, than he most likely would have had he lived to be 100 years old.

Go Jeremiah, go!

Jeremiah 1:4-6
The word of the Lord came to me, saying, "Before I formed you in the womb I knew you, before you were born I set you apart; I appointed you as a prophet to the nations."

SUFFER NOT IN SILENCE

While the word "Lamentations" does not sound like a good read, this book of the Bible is an important one. It shows us how lament, prayer and grief are crucial in our relationship and journey with the Lord. We are encouraged to **not suffer in silence,** but voice our pain and vent our feelings. Suffering often makes us question God's character and love for us – which He wants us to feel free to do. By voicing our confusion, we begin to process our emotions, and **seek God** for answers. And He will be faithful to show up every time. In this, our hearts soften and we are able to draw closer to the One **who longs to comfort and give us hope.**

Having a sense of peace and a hope about the children I lost through miscarriages did not come until I got real with God and vocalized my pain and disappointment. The answers I found in His Word comforted me and renewed my faith rather than tore it apart. Creating a blog not only gave me an outlet to express my pain, but to my surprise, opened a door for me to touch a community of people who shared in my sorrow.

A few months after starting the blog I met Dave, the director of a local crisis pregnancy center. He had a table set up on the patio at my church, providing information and volunteer opportunities within their organization. He was inspired by my story and asked if I would be willing to start a miscarriage support group. I told him I had never heard of such a thing, and he said, "That's because it doesn't exist." When clients from their center fail to see a heartbeat on the ultrasound monitor or women call in asking for help to cope with a miscarriage, he sends them a pamphlet and a prayer, but that's all he can offer. My heart broke for these women. I told Dave that if the church was willing to host such a class, I would lead it.

Not only was the church willing to host, they even blocked out time and space on their master calendar for the class to be a six-week course, and to be offered three times throughout the year. Wow! Talk about trust - I didn't even have a curriculum written yet. Plus, as there had never been such a class on this subject, the need for it was merely assumed.

When someone I respect sees a specific strength in me and asks me to walk in it, I rarely say no. To me, it would be like saying no to God. So I take it seriously, and if fear is the only thing holding me back, I push through it. **Self-confidence is not necessary when I have God-confidence**. With that, I sat down to work on the curriculum for this quickly approaching class.

The first step to writing anything is knowing who your audience is. Honestly, I didn't even know if I'd have an audience. Miscarrying a child is often viewed as a "private matter," so perhaps no one would even come. I went back to my foundational verse:

Jeremiah 1:5

Before I formed you in the womb I knew you, before you were born I set you apart. I appointed you as a prophet to the nations.

As I pondered this, I felt a nudge to read on. Here is Jeremiah's response to the Lord's appointment for him:

Jeremiah 1:6

"Ah Sovereign Lord, I do not know how to speak; I am only a child."

Wow, seriously?! It was as if my very own thoughts and apprehensions had been recorded in this most ancient of books. I totally get you, Jeremiah. I couldn't wait to hear what the Lord had to say to ~~me~~ him next.

Jeremiah 1:7,8

But the Lord said to me, "Do not say, 'I am only a child'. You must go to everyone I send you to and say whatever I command you. Do not be afraid of them, for I am with you," declares the Lord

Hmmm, I never asked to be heard by anyone but Him, and much like Jeremiah, God sent the people over to my blog. Okay, I was feeling a little better. God's in charge of sign-ups and if Jeremiah shouldn't fear the nations of people, I should not be fearful of a possible room full of them.

There was just one other thing discouraging me: Every mom in that room would have had her own unique experience at different stages in their pregnancies. What would I say to a woman who lost her baby at full term? How do I speak the words that individually, these moms need to hear? Well, I kept reading...

Jeremiah 1:9,10

Then the Lord reached out his hand and touched my mouth and said to me, "Now I have put my words in your mouth. See, today I appoint you over nations and Kingdoms to uproot and tear down, to destroy and overthrow, to build and to plant."

I know these words I was reading were said to Jeremiah, but isn't it possible that God intended them for all who are willing to lead in His Name? I think so. Well, at least that's what I was holding onto as I took on this call to leadership. And as it turns out, I didn't actually need my own words, I had God's Word, and the testimony of how He turned my hurt into hope. I just shared some wisdom from the Bible in addition to my story and the 11 people that came to that first class felt comfortable to share theirs too. I couldn't give them a cure for their broken hearts, but I could give them a safe place to express an inexpressible pain, voice their confusion, and process their emotions of anger, fear, shame, and eventually peace. I had them write God a letter and encouraged them not to hold back. The Lord already knows what is in your heart and mind, you might as well let it all out. And by not suffering in silence, you create room in your heart for peace and hope. You can trust Him; for He also knows what it's like to lose a child and to one day hold Him again in Heaven.

Lamentations 3:19-23
I remember my affliction and my wandering, the bitterness and the gall. I well remember them, and my soul is downcast within me. Yet this I call to mind and therefore I have hope: Because of the Lord's great love we are not consumed, for His compassions never fail. They are new every morning; great is your faithfulness.

SHEPHERD JANITORIAL SERVICES

In the Book of Ezekiel, we are presented with a metaphor of God removing our hardened heart of stone and giving us a new, softer heart of flesh through His Spirit. This concept is depicted not just in Ezekiel, but referred to throughout the Bible. One example of this is found in Ezekiel 34 **as a warning to shepherds not to care more for themselves than the sheep that the Lord has put in their charge**.

....

Mid-way through 2012, I began volunteering as a counselor at The Pregnancy Resource Clinic. I was trained over a three-month period to counsel women experiencing unplanned pregnancies, who came to this clinic seeking options, advice and early pregnancy services - with full confidentiality and at no cost to them. The clinic offered free pregnancy tests and ultrasounds after a one-on-one meeting that educated them about their options. The Gospel was presented to them in love, and many lives were saved – physically and spiritually. There were often women who came in just for the free test and a mind set on terminating if their pregnancy test was positive. While this option would be discussed, it would not be performed. The Pregnancy Clinic holds a pro-woman/pro-child approach in which both lives are valued and encouraged.

Some women left right after taking a pregnancy test, never to be seen again. But then there were women like the one who came back for a free ultrasound a few weeks later with her boyfriend. Her test had been positive and she left with the intent to make an appointment with Planned Parenthood to terminate the pregnancy. Her boyfriend insisted on seeing for himself if there was really a baby before he shelled out $400 for an abortion. Upon hearing the heartbeat and seeing his developing child, he literally passed out in the ultrasound room.

The couple left in tears, but not before the boyfriend could say, "Thank you, you just saved our baby's life."

The Pregnancy Clinic was so effective at loving the lost that they expanded their facility, changed their name to Open Arms Pregnancy Clinic, and found a larger more accessible

location. The week of their move, I received an email informing me that instead of seeing clients that week, they were asking if volunteers would come into the new building to help clean and prepare before the move. Initially, I was excited about helping Open Arms make this transition in whatever way that I could. When the day of my volunteering came, I packed up some cleaning supplies from under my own dish-filled sink and headed out the door. I decided not to share with my husband that I would be cleaning instead of counseling, given the current condition of our own home. As I drove, I noticed a little seed of doubt lined with bitterness was beginning to form within me. (Why would I possibly go help someone else clean when I have cleaning of my own to catch up on? The fact that I feel the need to hide this from my husband tells me that I should perhaps not be doing this. There are actually people out there who have "the gift of cleaning." God is fully aware that I am not one of them. Yeah, this is bound to be a decision I will regret!)

In the background of this growing seed, I could hear a recorded teaching CD I had left playing in my car. It was the voice of Cindy, the leader from the Genesis study I was taking. She was talking about creation and how nothing God creates is an accident. My mind then turned to the unborn, who (much like my own heavenly little one) have a purpose and a Divine Creator. My little seed of doubt had become dormant by the time I parked my car and willingly entered the building. Walking into the new office, the smell of fresh paint filled my nostrils as I extended a hug to Debi, the Director of Open Arms.

"I'm so glad you could come," she said. And with that, I wondered what important task awaited me. "If you could fill your bucket with soap and water, I'll have you start by washing the walls in the bathroom."

Her words were like Miracle Grow to my no-longer-dormant-seed. But being a first-born, the desire to please others always puts me on autopilot. So, there I stood on a step stool, dipping my rag into clear soapy water. By stretching my open arms, I was able to reach into places where dust had accumulated and perhaps had never felt the touch of such simple cleaning power. I then became aware that this was the 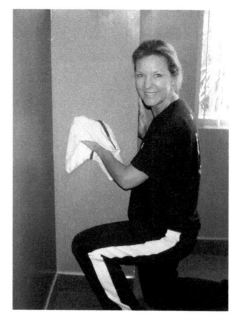 very room that women take the life-changing test. Despite whether it's a "+" experience or a "-" experience, they will leave this room with a whole new view than the one they walked in with.

I suddenly felt the beating of my own heart. I swallowed hard to fight back the lump that was growing in my throat. I realized that just like the Genesis message stated on the car ride over, God had not put me here on accident. It wasn't my cleaning skills that He desired; it was my ability to see beyond the dusty walls. He wanted someone interceding for these scared and confused new moms. He wanted me! So for the next two hours, I stayed at Open Arms and proceeded to do other seemingly menial tasks with the happiest of hearts. I even had time to go home before picking up carpool to tend to my own dish-filled sink. That day, I learned that caring for someone can take on many different forms. The act of taking my eyes off of myself and investing my time, energy, and prayers into another who is confused and in need of direction is what it means to shepherd. Sometimes we may not even know who we are caring for, but God does. He is our ultimate Shepherd. He knows all the sheep by name. He is even willing to leave His flock temporarily to find and aid that one lost lamb. What an honor it is for us to do a version of the same.

Ezekiel 34:2b

"This is what the Sovereign Lord says: Woe to you shepherds of Israel who only take care of yourselves! Should not shepherds take care of the flock?"

FAITH ON A POPSICLE STICK

The Israelite's captivity in Babylon was full of challenges that tested their faith. *Daniel in the lion's den and Shadrach, Meshach, and Abednego in the fiery furnace* are just two examples of immense hope that motivates such faithfulness. All four of these **men stood firm in their unpopular practices and belief in the one true God**, despite the persecution and danger that would result from it. The test of their faith was great, but the reward for their faithfulness was even greater.

....

I've never forgotten Thanksgiving 2001, when we all gathered as usual at my parents' house for an early evening feast. The standard crew was there: my sister and her husband, my two grandmothers, a couple of old friends of the family, my husband and I, our two boys ages four and one, and of course my parents. Over the years, a tradition had begun where just before eating the Thanksgiving meal we would go around the table and each person would say one thing they were thankful for. Phrases like "my health," "my family," and "everyone here tonight"  were typically shared year after year. Well, being a teacher who loves coming up with creative and fun ideas, I took it upon myself to put a new spin on this little family tradition. I got crafty with my kids and we used small, brown pom-poms to make a turkey head and glued it on to a small terracotta pot. We then colored popsicle sticks and placed them inside the pot to act as "feathers." Before dinner, Blake and I had each guest pick out a popsicle stick and asked them to write what they were thankful for on it. The idea was to stay anonymous until everyone was gathered at the table, at which point we would each pick a random stick and guess who said what. So far my idea was a hit, and everyone was looking forward to playing the game. Just before we sat down, I grabbed one more stick and a sharpie and quietly whispered, "Blake, what are you thankful for?" Without hesitation he said, "I'm thankful that Jesus died on the cross for my sins."

Wow! As a mom, I was amazed at my four-year-old's pure heart and sound conviction. (I mean I was expecting something more like "my computer games" or "pizza.") But somehow, as I held the marker in my hand, I couldn't bring myself to write down his response. You see my family has never been open about religion. Growing up we would always say a rote prayer at dinner and a "Now I lay me down to sleep..." before bed. But any kind of relationship or theologies about God was something we kept to ourselves. When my sister and I became teens, my parents started watching the news during dinner and nobody tucked us into bed anymore so praying together as a family just stopped. It was as if prayer was something you only do out loud when you're a kid (or at least have a kid). I suppose once the kids are grown, it's a personal choice and everyone privately does their own prayer - that is if they choose to. We never actually discussed why we stopped, but this was my unconfirmed understanding.

Once I had a family of my own, I decided to be more intentional about God in our home and we prayed prayers that were more like a conversation with the Lord than a chant. But tonight, we weren't in our home and I wasn't sure how the rest of the family would react to such a bold statement. This popsicle stick was bound to make some people uncomfortable. And what would people think of me? I'm sure some would secretly believe I put Blake up to it. (After all, I'm his mom and I can't even believe he said that.)

"Why aren't you writing anything, Mommy?" Blake asked.

I had no answer. Therefore, I had no other choice but to write down what he said and mix it in with the rest. Whose idea was this again?

So there we all sat, each holding another's wooden stick. I had no idea who had Blake's stick, but I had plenty of ideas on how awkward this was going to be. With each thankful phrase that was read, I gave a little sigh of relief. Smiles were shared, guesses were given, and now we came to the last stick reader: my dad. Due to the process of elimination, everyone knew whose stick he was holding. Strong and proud he read, "I am thankful that Jesus died on the cross for my sins." What happened next will continue to humble me for the rest of my life. My dad looked straight across the table into my son's pure, innocent eyes and said, "Yes Blake, Jesus died for all of our sins." From under the table, I felt the tight squeeze of my husband's hand on my leg and I knew he too couldn't believe what had just happened. Next there was a second or two of silence and then someone said "Cheers!" We clanked our glasses together and the moment was gone. But not for me. I bit my lip as I tried to hold back my tears. I felt disappointed in myself for hesitating before I wrote, and for selfishly worrying what others may think. I couldn't believe I almost robbed God of this beautiful moment of bringing Jesus to our Thanksgiving table. I wanted to find my popsicle stick and change my answer to, "I am thankful for this very moment, when my dad boldly proclaimed Christ as Savior to his grandson and anyone else who was listening."

As Matthew 18:4 so perfectly states, Therefore whoever humbles himself like this child is the greatest in the Kingdom of Heaven. I pray I grow in spiritual maturity to have the child-like faith needed to be so bold and unashamed.

Daniel 4:2

It is my pleasure to tell you about the miraculous signs and wonders that the Most High God has performed for me.

A CALL TO LOVE

Hosea was a man called by God to represent **God's love for Israel despite Israel's rebellion and dismissal of Him**. In this book of the Bible, Hosea was to take and love a lost woman. In this chapter of my book, I am to leave and love a lost man. God may call us to love in ways that don't feel comfortable, but His ways are not often our ways. That's where faith and trust in God come in.

....

Dear Former Husband,

I am writing you a letter you will probably never read, but I'm not writing it for you; I'm writing it for me. I have prayed for you many times, but never with a heart as soft as the one I currently have.

Father God, please help him to feel your love. A love that is not humanly possible. A love that says: I know everything about you and still my commitment to you will not waiver. I created you and then watched your every move, from conception until now. There is no action or thought you have hidden from Me. I know it all, and yet you are still My child and I'm not giving up on you. I am always here, just call on Me.

While we were married, I prayed for the Lord to give me a heart like His for you: *Help me to love him unconditionally and accept him for who he is.*

But your desire for divorce came anyway.

Looking back, it was really difficult for both of us to be unequally yoked, as our vast viewpoints made a partnership near impossible. But in the depths of my heart, <u>there is still love</u>.

In the early months after our divorce, I fought this desire to still love you. But it is no wonder I felt this way; God had actually been answering my prayer to love you unconditionally and not ignoring it. At times, I beat myself up for allowing you to occupy a piece of my heart that I so desperately would like back. But I no longer wish to push this emotion away or try to deny its existence. Instead I will identify it for what it really is: a Christ-like love. A love that says, "I have every reason to reject you as you have rejected me, but I don't."

I recall shortly after we were separated, I came back to the house to get a few things. As I walked through the garage, I noticed your car had a large plastic #1 on the roof above the driver's door, like something a Service Station would use. Upon entering the house, I inquired about it. You looked at me like I was crazy and said you had no idea what I was talking about. I convinced you to walk back out to the garage  with me, and you were shocked to see it. You said that you had gotten an oil change and then ran two more errands before coming home- somehow never once noticing this large plastic service number, magnetized to the hood of your car. I didn't get it. How do you possibly miss that? How do you not see something so obvious? It was as if God whispered in my ear, "He is truly blind to the consequences of ending your marriage that you can clearly see." It was at that moment I realized that there was nothing I could do. Our scope of vision was not the same.

God's Word (Luke 15 &17) showed me how to love you: I love you like a lost lamb, who wandered off course due to lack of direction.

I love you like the prodigal son, who took his half of the inheritance and left seeking greater happiness. I love you like a soldier who yelled blasphemous statements toward me and pierced my side; forgiving you - for you know not what you do.

I no longer feel anguish over you. I feel the permission to let you go, and best of all, I feel the grace to still love you, in spite of it all.

Hosea 3:1
Go, Love (him) as the Lord loves the Israelites, though they turn to other gods.

OH, MERCY ME!

The Day of the Lord is dreadful, who can endure it? This is not only a verse from the Book of Joel, but also the theme of God's forthcoming judgment. Thankfully, God longs to show mercy to those who seek it and confess their sins. We are called to **rend our hearts and return to God,** not as an outward adornment – but as true inner genuine change. For the Lord's mercy and love is even more powerful than His judgment.

My best friend Toni C. and I like to quote **Joel 2:25** to each other: **The Lord will repay you for the years the locusts have eaten**. It's just our way to offer a smile and an encouragement as we each attempt to find a new normal after divorce. God is going to give us something so wonderful in our future that it will make up for the precious time we invested in relationships that failed. We seem to quote this verse more often around the holidays. There is nothing worse than foregoing either Christmas Eve or Christmas morning with your once-upon-a-time family. The math is easy: two days for celebrating Christmas and two parents to celebrate with. But oh how I long to go back and have both Christmas Eve and Christmas Day with my children. That family-togetherness the locusts have now eaten.

It was the second Christmas after my divorce. I was looking forward to spending Christmas Eve dining with my boys at my parents' house as we traditionally always have. A few days before, I picked up Ryan from his parkour gym. As we drove home he dropped a bomb on me. "This year we are having Christmas morning at Dad's girlfriend's house, so Blake and I are going to leave right after dinner on Christmas Eve so we can be there early with Dad when her kids wake up to do presents and stockings."

I don't think Ryan meant to hurt me, but with a knife twisting back and forth in my heart, I wasn't in a place to offer anyone grace. To put it calmly, I completely lost it! I went on and on about MY time and MY holiday, and MY feelings. I wasn't just mad-angry, I was mad-crazy. So much so that as I approached the intersection, I never even registered that the light was red. In fact it didn't even dawn on me that I was running a red light until I began to spew out more harsh words to Ryan sitting in the passenger seat. As my head turned to look at him, all I could see were headlights blinding my vision. I heard a continual honk of someone's horn but never even put my foot on the brake, and thank God I didn't because based off the g-force I felt behind me, the truck with the headlights would have hit us. Now on the safe side of the intersection, I realized what just happened. There had to have been angels surrounding my car for us to drive through unscathed. I pulled the car over and looked into my teenager's crystal blue eyes and hugged him like I knew I could have lost him.

At some point after that moment, I did indeed rend my heart and return to God. I was keenly aware of the reality that I could have easily spent my Christmas Eve next to a hospital bed, praying over my son's broken body and pleading for God to spare his life; that is if he had even survived the accident. For days, I could not stop thanking God for His mercy. I was fully to blame for my reckless, selfish anger and deserved consequences way worse than children leaving early on "my day." In fact, come Christmas Eve, we ate dinner at 3 p.m. and the boys were excused to leave for their dad's right after dessert. I hugged them goodbye from the porch and told them "drive safely," for there was plenty of time, no need to rush. It turned out to be the most thankful Christmas I've ever had. I walked back inside realizing that today wasn't "my day." It was the Day of the Lord, the day that God made a way for me and all those who recognize His love and mercy through the gift of His son Jesus, to be saved.

Joel 2:32

And everyone who calls on the name of the Lord will be saved; for on Mount Zion and in Jerusalem there will be deliverance, as the Lord has said, even among the survivors whom the Lord calls.

LOVE DIFFERENT

The prophet Amos speaks harshly and boldly about **God's call to justice.** The hypocrisy of God's people elevating themselves as higher than those who are poor, or less powerful, or whatever the difference, is brought to light. **Justice is to flow like a river.** In the Book of Amos, the Israelite families were reminded of the measures God had taken in the past to get their attention, yet they still did not turn to Him. These sins of self-righteousness and entitlement are not just unique to the Israelites from long ago. Many people today still find it challenging to love those who are different from them. I know this full well.

....

It took me a very long time to learn this simple truth: Different isn't wrong; it's just different. Growing up, I may have been labeled "a good girl," but my propensity to place judgment on others was not good at all. The sheltering and protection that was provided for me throughout my childhood was done out of love, but as a result it made it difficult for me to embrace love outside of my bubble. I did not live in a neighborhood or go to a school where other races, religions, or alternative lifestyles were highly visible. I actually recall being somewhat fearful of people who looked or acted differently than me. My little world was the standard, anything that veered away from it "just wasn't right." As ashamed as I am to admit it, this was my raw truth.

As I got older and began to add new, eye-opening experiences to my repertoire, my rigid viewpoints began to weaken. But I never really saw my remaining "blindspots" until I was blessed with a child who had a God-given gift to embrace all things different. From a very early age, Ryan was captivated by ideas and people that were different from him. At times I reprimanded him for rudely staring at strangers, but I quickly learned that he wasn't really being rude – he was simply fascinated. Here are some examples:

- When standing in line for a movie, I couldn't pull his attention away from the man ahead of us speaking to his friend in another language. Ryan finally broke away from their conversation and asked, "Mommy, how do I learn to talk like that?"

- Waiting on the freeway off-ramp for the light to change, I did every- thing in my power to not make eye contact with the homeless man standing outside to my left, but Ryan was fixated on him. And after the light finally turned green, he asked, "If I make him a sack lunch, will you drive me back here to give it to him?" (Which I did and as Ryan boldly handed him the bag, the man's grateful smile melted my hardened heart.)

- When Ryan started acting for the studios, they used "stand-in actors" for when the lighting and sound crew needed to set the angles for the next scene. In the case of child actors, adults who are little people of their same height are hired to stand in for them. Ryan's "stand-in" was named Brooke and he was in awe of her. After meeting her for the first time, he tried to process her uniqueness as we walked back to his dressing room - "So Mom, she's actually an adult but she's little like me – do you think I could be a little person when I grow up?" He was a bit disappointed when I told him that it's a specialness you have to be born with. He loved looking eye-to-eye with Brooke and chatting with her in between takes. As a curious six-year-old, he would ask her questions that were perfectly understandable, "I'm not big enough to go on Space Mountain yet, but can you go on – 'cause you're not a kid?" Ryan felt so sad to learn that she will never get to go on big rollercoasters because the height requirement is a strict safety factor. During the six-month shoot, I too grew close to Brooke. She told me that few child actors are as accepting and befriending as Ryan was.

She tried to give me credit as his mom, but the truth was he was my example when it came to befriending others. I soon learned Brooke and I had much in common and she quickly became my favorite friend on set.

- When Ryan was seven years old we hosted Abby, a Ugandan teacher, in our home for a short time. Ryan was instantly drawn to her, always gently touching her dark skin and unintention- ally making her laugh with his bold statements. He loved her  strong British-Ugandan accent and had many long chats with her. Once, she asked him if his teacher was very old. Ryan responded to what he heard, "Oh yes, she is very odd." Abby laughed and told him she would very much like to meet this teacher one day. So the next morning at school, Ryan made arrangements to bring Abby in for Share Day, and later that week proudly introduced her to his oddly wonderful first grade teacher and his classmates. To this day, I still consider Abby one of my dearest friends. She hosted me in her home when I went to Africa and we continue to write and visit on social media.

I loved seeing people and situations through Ryan's eyes. He never thought about being politically correct or if his words or actions would be misunderstood. He just took a sincere interest in others and fully appreciated the parts that were different, and with that he was always well-received. He paved the way for me to comfortably and boldly befriend those that I normally would shy away from. I realize now it's not that I was prejudiced against people - I just was fearful of saying the wrong thing or being misunderstood. Keeping quietly to myself felt safe and easy, but that's not at all what God intends for us. Over time I began to grasp this concept, to the point that I don't recognize that ignorant, uneasy girl I was before. Keep reading. My own, love different, transformation is coming up in the Book of Zechariah.

Amos 5:24
But let justice roll on like a river, righteousness like a
never-failing stream!

ROAD TO REDEMPTION

Obadiah, whose name means "servant of the Lord," had a vision
regarding the divine judgment over the nation of Edom. Edom had
a shared ancestry with Israel; these two tribes came from the line
of Jacob and Esau. Much like the strained relationship between these
two brothers that we learn about back in Genesis, these two nations
followed suit. **Edom's pride and betrayal eventually lead to their
fall, but God brought healing and hope for a better future for Israel.**
This may be the shortest book of the Bible, but it manages to fill me
with appreciation and hope for my own tribe too.

I never met my dad's dad. He lived
in England all his life and died when
I was seven years old. I remember
the telegram being delivered to our
home. I knew the letter must be
important for a mail carrier to knock
on our front door and ask for my dad's
signature. As he read over the notice,

he gave in to my obvious curiosity. "It's a note from England letting me
know that my dad has passed away," he informed me. "Are you going
to cry?" I asked him. He told me no, that he and his dad were not close.
I assured my dad that if he died, I would cry a lot. He responded, "Well I
would hope so." And we never spoke about it again.

Throughout my young life, all I really gathered about my dad's father
was that he was a gambler, an alcoholic, a verbally abusive husband and
father, and a brilliant journalist/writer. I think I was always so shocked by
his first three attributes that I never paid much attention to the last one.

I was told my Nana divorced him because "enough was enough." (Good for you, Nana!) She was the most wonderful, loving woman in all of the world. In fact, I aspire to be like her. The idea of someone treating her poorly and taking her

love and kindness for granted really upset me, so I chose not to think about it. Plus, Nana was re-married to Granddad, and he came into our family way before I did, so there was never a void of something amiss in our clan.

It was during our recent move that I stumbled upon a book called "The Art of Story-Writing" written by Les Preston. It had always been kept on the shelf in the secretary desk that my dad built, but I had never once seen it taken out. This book now lives on a shelf in my bedroom at our new house. I knew one day I'd be writing a book full of stories and the fact that I have a blood relative who wrote a book on story-writing, made me think I should one day crack it open and see what was inside. So

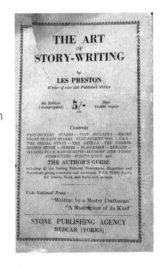

a few weeks ago, thanks to a power outage, my mom and I brought out the battery-operated lanterns she had proudly purchased years ago from her Publishers Clearing House days and sat down together to read it. To my surprise, there were some papers that fell out as I opened the book. My dad had kept the telegram from 1978 as well as two letters that were also stuffed inside. The first was dated "11 April 1969," from Les to my Dad. I couldn't make out much of the handwriting, but from what I gathered, he wrote mostly on himself;

some horses he had bet on, and possibly some updates on local soccer leagues. Given the date, I realized my parents would have been married for just six months, yet the letter gives no mention of his bride or inquires about married life. I wondered if he even knew of their union, or perhaps he felt ashamed to mention a life event that he failed so miserably at.

I asked my mom if she remembered anything about that time. She said she didn't know my dad had been sent that letter, but the following year, in 1970 (the year before I was born), my dad took her on a trip to Yorkshire, England to see where he grew up. She said they popped in to visit Les; a quiet man who spoke no more than six words to her. He took them to his favorite pub where he was well known by all. They had a drink together and that was that – it would be the last time my dad would see his dad. Even after receiving word of his stroke in that 1978 telegram, my dad did not rush back to England. Instead, he arranged for a friend living near Les' hometown to take care of the cremation and clearing out of his flat (which my mom recalled was already practi-

cally empty the eight years prior when they had visited). It is such a shame that he lived a life that lost sight of how important family was and in the end, died alone. I thought about my own dad's death and all the people who showed up to his celebration of

life ceremony. We tried to keep it small and intimate, but he was so well-respected and loved by so many that people just kept showing up. Four years after my dad's passing, my sister and I would fly to Australia along with our Aunt Linda (my dad's half-sister, from Nana's better marriage). Together the three of us would surprise my dad's older sister, Aunty Vonny, for her 90th birthday celebration. The large banquet room was filled to capacity with her five children, her many grandchildren, as well as her great grandchildren, in addition to more extended family and friends. Aunty Vonny sobbed as she clenched my sister and me in her arms. It wasn't my dad, her brother Alan, but it was the next best thing. Both of these well-attended events were quite a testament to the difference the power of a mother's love can make, combined by the faithfulness of a Heavenly Father, who is ready to take over when an earthly parent fails you.

The second letter that fell out of "The Art of Story-Writing" was one that my Aunty Vonny wrote to my Dad shortly after Les' passing. I cried at their beautiful sibling relationship even though they lived continents apart. She shared some memories from their early years as a family. She recalled their dad would tell them stories from the Bible and take them to the beach to find sea coal. He also sang and played the banjo. One night during World War II, air raid sirens warned that the German planes were overhead and ready to drop bombs on the nearby Steelworks. Les played his banjo and sang songs to drown out the terrible noise, making their reality a little less scary. Her letter warmed my heart and gave me hope that my own children would be able to reflect on their special memories of being young together. Like my dad and his sister, Ryan and Blake were also ages 13 and 15 when my husband and I divorced. I pray that my boys will also grow to value family and commitment despite not seeing that unity in us, their parents. Aunty Vonny's letter became a personal and timely beacon of hope for me.

"The Art of Story-Writing" was written in England in 1941, so the book itself wasn't an easy read for Mom and I -but we did very much enjoy it. In fact, I recognized some similar word choices and writing styles between Les' short stories and my own. That was pretty special for me.

I could sense a tender side to this cold and removed man that I should have been able to call my grandpa. How very sad that he could express this passion in his writings for strangers, but lost the ability to express such love to his own family. May I inherit his passion for writing, with the added ability to generously love beyond the written word. There are actually some beautiful redemptive qualities in all of this for me. I suppose it shaped his former wife and children into the strong, loving, and faithful people I got to benefit from in my own life - so for that I am grateful to him. I see the family that my nana, aunt, and dad went on to create as the rainbow after the storm.

It turns out that mine isn't the first book dedicated to my dad. At the ages of 9 and 11, my dad and his sister were also recipients of such an honor. Les writes of their "unshakable faith" in his dedication,

a phrase I've always identified with and have often used in my own writing. Perhaps these are words that my dad brings out in others. Anyone can write a book, but to have a book dedicated to you (twice even) – well, that makes you truly inspirational.

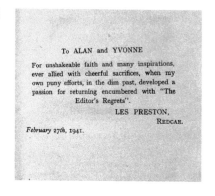

To ALAN and YVONNE

For unshakeable faith and many inspirations, ever allied with cheerful sacrifices, when my own puny efforts, in the dim past, developed a passion for returning encumbered with "The Editor's Regrets".

LES PRESTON,
REDCAR.

February 27th, 1941.

Oh how I wish my dad were still here to share in this story with me. But I am grateful for the information that I have recently come across, and that I still have my Aunty Vonny: the reigning matriarch of our beautiful tribe. Praise God for bringing healing and hope to a family that I am proud to call my own.

Obadiah vs. 17

But on Mount Zion will be deliverance; it will be holy, and the house of Jacob will possess its inheritance.

ME, AN AUTHOR?

The story of Jonah is surely a familiar one from the Bible. Jonah tries to **run away from what God has planned** for him and ends up spending three days in the belly of a whale, then is spat out on the very land where **God had appointed him** to preach. Jonah's time isolated inside of that whale gave him perspective, wisdom, and motivation to finally obey the Lord. While many find this story a bit too far-fetched to be true, I believe it and find its message extremely relatable, not just in my own journey but on a global level as well.

....

While this chapter is exactly halfway through the Bible (as well as my book), it's the one I chose to write last. I waited until the end because I didn't know if I would stick with it and follow through with what the Lord put on my heart so many years ago. Like Jonah, I was clear on what God was stirring in me to do, but I ran from it. The desire to write a book has been within me for some time (If you are anything like me and you skipped over the intro and headed straight into Chapter One, you may want to take a minute to go back and read that now). It's not that I didn't want to write a book, it's that I didn't think I could actually do it. So I always had an excuse ready to go: my kids keep me too busy, I'm working full-time again, my marriage is falling apart, I have a ministry to run, my dad's passed and my mom needs me, I need to focus on dating after divorce because once I'm 50 I'm sure it'll be a challenge. But with each passing year, God never took my desire to write away, instead He just used my excuses and gave me more to write about.

I remember telling God years ago that unless He could somehow hide me away for at least six months without a social life, a job, or my family to worry about, I didn't see how authoring a book would be a possibility. And God, in His infinite wisdom, knew that Covid-19 would one day enter our world, quickly remove all of my excuses and give me the very sheltering I had asked for. Having just moved to a house that made caring for my mom much easier, staying isolated at home in order to protect her health, plus spending far less time with my adult sons who did not want to expose their Mimi to outside elements, pretty much met my terms of negotiation with the Lord. But He even threw in a bonus to keep me from getting distracted: it was nearly impossible to date with a highly contagious illness looming through our planet. It didn't matter that I was 49 (or "forty-fine" as my girlfriends and I like to say), the unlikely chance of meeting a great guy via Zoom or in the grocery store with masks covering our faces, only shows how determined the Lord truly

was to have all my attention and see this through together.

God even accommodated me with my very own whale. After a few unsuccessful attempts to sit in a chair at my desk, I decided to move my home office to my queen-sized bed. Compared to Jonah's contemplating quarters, God truly was treating me like a queen. In recent years my lower back has not been my friend, so sitting or standing in one position too long can be debilitating. Getting up from my "throne" to help my mom every couple of hours, gave my legs and spine the continual stretching that was needed. I ordered a cute little bed tray that was designed more for a laptop than for a breakfast, and propped up pillows all around me to keep me comfortable. As you can probably surmise from my first 28 chapters, many of these stories required me to tap into an array of emotions. I did not have to fight the temptation to curl up under the covers, for I already was there. While revisiting areas of my past, I allowed myself to feel deeply, go there fully, and be as authentic as possible to what was happening in that moment and what my response was to it. I was surprised to learn how often my outward and inward responses did not align. It humbled me to realize how little I actually knew, yet how much God wanted to show me. If I had written this book while my boys were still living under my roof, it would not have been as easy to access the pain I felt when they weren't with me. If I had written this book before my miscarriage, or my divorce, or my dad's death, not only would those stories be missing from it, but other stories would lack the depth of understanding and peace from God that each experience taught me. So while it did take me 10 years to finally sit down (or in my case, lounge) and make this dream a reality, it wasn't too late. In fact, it was the perfect time for me to stop and truly reflect on every aspect of my life and honestly seek God in writing my story with Him in the starring role. Sometimes I spent all day writing, only to later recall different details as I slept, or went for a walk, or heard from a sermon, or learned during a Bible study discussion. I constantly revisited stories until I was confident in their accuracy and the explanation of God's power within them. I couldn't help but wonder if this might be how the authors of God's Word felt as they would write and recall events. There are times I go back and read what I wrote and realize those words were more from God than they were from me. Many people have told me that this often happens to them as well when they sit quietly and journal or pray. I found other's insights invaluable to me. Any story that included someone other than myself, I would track them down (thank you, social media), email them the unedited version of "our" story and ask for their blessing as well as any further clarity on this experience through their eyes. At times I would change a name or two to make the person more comfortable with me sharing something so personal, but the story itself was accurate or became accurate after discussing it further with them. Oftentimes people would recall details that had slipped my mind and now made the story even more beautiful. Some even sent me photos that they had taken from our shared experience. My boys found the stories of their childhood endearing and humorous, but worked with me on what I was allowed to share once my reflections hit middle school and beyond.

My prayer has always been that each of my stories speak the truth in love and give God the glory. That is why I knew I would have to self-publish. "It's Real to Me" is my personal, God-ordained book of moments throughout life where God has clearly shown Himself to me. There is no way I could allow a publishing agency to take control of that. Instead, God brought Toni Purry to mind. She was not only a fellow sister in Christ but a successful, self-published author. I hired Toni to guide me through every stage of the process and not only do I now have a book, but a strategy and a platform for it to reach others.

So here you go world: my book of obedience. I never imagined actually getting this far, so I have no expectations on how it will be received by others. But much like Jonah, my instructions were to simply tell, and in finishing this chapter, I have done just what was asked of me. What I hadn't anticipated was how much I would enjoy the process of writing, be blessed by connecting with family, friends, and acquaintances whom I share these stories with, and be eternally grateful for this imperfect life that has allowed me to experience the Lord in so many perfect ways.

Jonah 2:8,9

"Those who cling to worthless idols turn away from God's love for them. But I, with shouts of grateful praise, will sacrifice to you. What I have vowed I will make good. I will say, 'Salvation comes from the Lord.' "

DEAR HOPEFUL

The Book of Micah teaches us that **God's ultimate purpose is not to destroy, but to save and redeem**. What that redemption looks like will become clearer over time. This book of the Bible is a wake-up call, stating there is nothing that can be done to undo the sins of the past. Redemption can only be experienced in the faith and hope of what is yet to come.

....

After nearly 19 years of working at my marriage, I didn't know how to stop. It was a piece of myself I didn't like. I really wanted to move on, but I could not let go of this part that still wanted to fight and make things right. Sandy, my wise and caring therapist, told me that that piece of me had a name and her name was Hopeful. She then gave me an assignment: Kim needs to write Hopeful a letter. There are things that Hopeful does not understand, but Kim does. Be gentle, for she is a part of you. We are not trying to get rid of Hope; we just want to redirect her.

 I found the assignment somewhat strange. But Sandy's methods have proven to be effective, so as soon as I got home, I cracked open my laptop and began to write my letter. I felt angry at myself for occasionally still wanting to go back and try harder. But the assignment was to be gentle, not angry. So, having a love for children, I decided to envision Hopeful as a little girl inside of me.

Dearest Hopeful,
Oh how I love your desire to bring out the very best in people. You have the ability to believe more in others than they might ever be capable of believing in themselves. Your heart is not for this marriage. Your heart is for the lost and broken of this world. Your former husband just happens to be one of those. As a Kindergarten teacher, you attached yourself to

the most challenging of students. Whether it was the shy pupil struggling to read aloud or the rambunctious one who couldn't sit still. They quickly became your projects to love into the very best 5-year-olds that they could possibly be. And at the end of the year, you, their parents, their classmates and other teachers would all see the growth that took place in those kids who once struggled. It made you so proud. For you stayed in there and fought for them, prayed for them, stretched them, and made them believe they could overcome whatever obstacles they faced. You did this with your own two boys as well. Today, you have two smart, confident, and respectful young men who are ready to take on the world. Your love and influence was a big part of that.

So, it makes perfect sense that you would want this for your ex-husband. You have invested this same heart for healing and success into a boy you have cherished since the ninth grade. You have staying power! You don't give up on people. Honestly, that's why you married him. You knew he had a confusing childhood, filled with emotional neglect and was a victim of multiple divorces. You were going to change that for him! You were going to show him what real, unconditional love and commitment looked like! And as a result he was going to feel secure and able to love like that in return. Except it didn't quite work out that way.

You have been trying to love him into happiness and contentment for nearly 30 years. It's so hard for you to walk away from what you have spent most of your life working towards. I get that! But I'm going to let you in on a little secret that will free you from this bondage....**He's not 5 years old**.

Years of trials and experiences have caused him to build a wall that, despite your commitment to moving, will never budge. The power of the Holy Spirit is the only way that wall will ever come down. You do not have, nor will you ever possess, the power to do this. You know the power exists, and you know how to put it into action… but you can't do it for him. He is the only one that can surrender to the love God has for him, who in turn can break down that wall.

I'm sorry that all those years invested in pushing and leaning in on this wall didn't even weaken the stronghold that the enemy had on it. But do not feel your efforts were completely wasted, for during those many years of persistence, you managed to strengthen your own body. You are not the weak vessel you once were. You are now equipped with muscles that you did not possess before. These will prove to be quite useful on the path before you.

So here we go, Miss Hopeful, one step at a time. We'll take it slow and see where God leads. I'm sure He will want you to exhibit some of that new strength along the way, so don't be surprised when disappointments arise. It's all part of His redemptive plan to get us right where we need to be. So let's walk forward and put our hope and trust in something that is still *yet to come*, rather than something that will *never* be.

We got this!

Your friend,
Kim

Micah 6:8

He has shown you, o mortal, what is good. And what does the Lord require of you? To act justly and to love mercy and to walk humbly with your God

PASS THE PEPPER

The Book of Nahum is yet another uncomfortable Old Testament read. Much like life, the Bible is not all good feels. This book of the Bible uses the fall of Nineveh as an example of God not allowing corruptible empires to endure, yet **providing refuge to those who are faithful to Him**. The fate of the nations will not be the fate of **God's faithful remnant**, but the path to overcoming oppression is a painful process in which God is grieved along with us.

....

My 5 Personal Stages of Divorce

Reel *(Jan. 2013 – May 2013)*
The pain, hurt, and rejection was unbearable. It honestly felt like someone ripped off my right arm and left me there to figure out how to survive. Constantly, throughout the days, I found myself giving my head a quick shake; in hopes of waking up from this nightmare. It can't be real! Divorce was something that happened to other people - people without love, people without hope, and people without God. I had an abundance of all three of those things. So how could this have happened to me? My mind was plagued with "should haves." I wanted desperately to go back in time and do things differently. Oh what I would have given for the chance to be a little kinder, to forgive a little quicker, and undo all of the adversities that led me to this moment. I felt like a failure: I failed my kids. I failed my God. I failed my church and my family. I failed all those people who looked up to me, convinced that I had the perfect life and marriage. Worst of all, I failed to have what it takes to be a wife that he was willing to fight for.

Deal *(June 2013 – Dec. 2013)*

Survival mode eventually kicked in. As a mother with children who still counted on me daily for care and guidance, I forced myself into this stage rather quickly. Birthdays, anniversaries, holidays, vacations - as much as I would have liked to skip over them, they came anyway. They were not the same, and deep down I knew they never would be. Nevertheless, I mustered up a smile and pretended all was good, while searching desperately for the wisdom of how to make this harsh reality work.

The life I had so beautifully mapped out had now been completely demolished, and rebuilding was impossible. Where once I saw decades in front of me, now I literally had no idea what tomorrow would look like. But one cannot worry about tomorrow, for like Manna from Heaven, we have only been given enough strength to make it through today.

At this point, I needed a diversion to get me through the confusion and fill the gaping hole in my heart. For some it is shopping, or clubbing, or eating, or exercising, or pouring oneself into another relationship. For others, it is reading God's Word, getting involved in church activities, seeking out ministries and friendships that will fill this void. For me, it was a combination of all these things. It seemed like every week I looked to a new distraction to escape the pain.

Feel *(Jan. 2014 – March 2014)*

Like an icepack, distractions eventually lose their cooling effect. As the numbing wore off, I began to feel the reality and the depth of what was happening. Allowing myself to take responsibility for my part, while holding my thoughts captive, to not run wild in the wrong direction was a balancing act of divine strength and courage. The story I wrote in my head was most likely very different from the actual story that was going on. It was a minute-by-minute battle to not compare what was happening within me to what I was seeing around me. My eyes focused on the happiness that others must feel, whether it was my former and his new, easygoing life, or those on social media who got to enjoy their healthy family unit with seemingly little to no effort.

I don't know how I would have gotten through this stage without a Savior to remind me that this was not my future, that there is an enemy that is constantly whispering lies in my ear. I knew deep down that it was okay to mourn my marriage and allow myself to grieve the list of losses that came with that. My therapist once told me: The hardest thing in life that one can go through is the death of a child, the second hardest is divorce, and after that - the death of a spouse. In time I began to understand this better. In divorce there is a form of death with the added elements of anger and rejection. I loved deeply in my marriage, so I am sure to hurt deeply in my divorce. It is best to stop and allow myself the need to feel this hurt, otherwise I will carry pieces of it around with me. As I live life, there will undoubtedly be moments that will trigger any neglected pain. I would rather endure as much of it as I can now, than invest in temporary painkillers the rest of my life, inevitably never to truly recover.

Kneel *(April 2014 – on going)*

The weight of carrying this hardship eventually brought me to my knees. I gave God my burden, for his yoke is light and can be used to haul much of the unneeded baggage away. It didn't happen overnight. Contrary to popular belief, time doesn't heal wounds, but God heals wounds in time.

An analogy that helped me understand the amount of time it would take to heal from this was picturing myself as salt in a transparent shaker. My ex-husband (still not an easy term to say) was the pepper in the shaker that accompanied me for over 20 years. With every experience we shared (whether it be a fond memory or a tough time) a dash of pepper was added to my salt. After years and years of pepper sifting through me, you can imagine how my salty identity may be hard to recognize.

During this kneeling process, the
pepper is removed. God takes out
one grain at a time, as to not remove
any of the saltiness that is me. At
this point, it was important for me
to stop praying for God to give me
what I wanted and start praying for

God to give me what I needed. The more time I invested in truly opening
up my heart to Him (rather than someone or something else), the more
room I gave Him to get to the pepper. Lots of *light and a clear path* were
needed in order to effectively grasp those dark spots that had lost their
flavor amidst the saltiness.

Heal *(a work in progress)*

While still on my knees, my salty goodness begins to come through.
I am more able to focus on my hopeful future than on my hopeless past.
When asked how I'm doing, I no longer paint myself as the victim on
this journey, but as a victor overcoming it. This is not the path I would
have chosen, but I accept that it is the path that I am on. This healing
could very well be a process I will continue to go through for the rest
of my life. Picturing my boys' graduations, weddings, the birth of
grandchildren no longer matches the picture of walking through these
experiences as a family unit. As sad as that sounds, I know I will be
equipped for those moments when they get here and not a moment
before. So I will focus on the present, and the blessings that today brings.

We live in an imperfect world and all of us are imperfect people.
Disappointments are guaranteed. My story is not over, but just beginning.
I have hope in an amazing God who is making me whole. Not only is my
salt clearly visible in the shaker, but it now contains more flavor than
ever before. I am now excited to embrace my new seasoning, as I walk
into my new season of life.

Nahum 1:7

The Lord is good, a refuge in times of trouble. He cares

for those who trust in Him.

GOD, I'M MAD AT YOU!

The Book of Habakkuk is unique in that instead of the author speaking boldly to the people on God's behalf, his harsh words are addressed to God Himself. Habakkuk spews his complaints at God for making decisions that are unfathomable. God listens and responds, making it clear that while He may use corruption for a greater purpose, He does not endorse it. **God is fighting for ultimate justice, even when we fail to see it.**

....

It had been just one week since our miscarriage. I was on my way out the door to attend my weekly women's Bible study. With a smile on my face, anxious to see my "sisters" who loved me, I gave my husband a quick kiss goodbye.

As I turned to leave he said, "I'm glad you're okay and everything, but I don't understand your pie-in-the-sky kind of attitude."

"What is that supposed to mean?" I asked.

He continued, " I don't get it! Why does a 16-year-old or a drug addict get to keep their babies and we don't? Doesn't God see what great parents we are? Why would he possibly take *our* baby?"

Of course my heart broke for him, but a part of me was glad that he was feeling something so passionate towards this child who God allowed to be taken from us. I wanted so badly to speak some enlightened words of wisdom, but what I had was inner peace – which was not the answer he needed to hear. You may be wondering, how it is that I have peace at this point and my husband does not. Well, to answer that, I need to go back four years to my previous miscarriage.

I was less than eight weeks along and hadn't even seen my doctor yet. But for me, the reality of having another child was already setting in: my boobs hurt, my jeans wouldn't button and I felt "gassy" and uncomfortable. Before each bite of food I would ask myself how this might affect the baby. My senses were heightened and I gladly avoided places with paint fumes or secondhand smoke. In short, I was reminded that I was "with child" dozens of times throughout the course of a day. Not so for my husband. Other than seeing a pink plus sign on a plastic stick and dealing with my complaints more often than my usual few days out of the month, life was just the same. We had never heard a heartbeat, seen an ultrasound photo, or even gotten an official due date. My miscarriage felt no different than a slightly heavier period and there wasn't any visual sign that there was ever an actual life within me. Nevertheless, I mourned and he didn't.

I think there were moments when he genuinely felt sad for me, but not for himself. Our experiences with this little life, thus far, were just so different. Looking back I can see how he never really had a chance to attach himself to the pregnancy and therefore it was as easy as waking up from a dream, realizing it wasn't real, and getting on with his day. I, on the other hand, can remember sneaking out to the backyard, laying on a lounge chair and bawling my eyes out. I didn't want to bother him with my unstable emotions. As much as he was right there next to me, I had never felt more alone. So, I took my anger to the source: God. Crying, yelling, and venting felt really good. I was mad at God and I needed to tell Him. *Why would You allow us to get pregnant after 3 years of praying if You knew You were just going to take this baby away from us? It's just mean and unfair. Clearly You want me to learn something from this struggle. Well couldn't You teach it to me without having to end this little life? Do You understand how much this hurts me?*

And I believe He's glad I did. He wants us to have an honest relationship with Him and sometimes that includes a side of us that isn't always pretty, but is very real. Instead of yelling back, He just listened. He waited until I had no more words or tears left. Then, once my emotions had quieted He opened my mind and spoke these words of truth to my heart: *Yes, I do understand how much it hurts to lose a Child.* (John 3:16) *Sometimes it is necessary in order for my ultimate plan to be fulfilled. I understand it is not clear to you from down there. But I have a different vantage point, and I can see what you cannot. Please trust me in this. Have I ever failed you before?*

Oh the sweetness of the Lord. How is it that He can humble me in such a loving way? When I allow myself to be still in His presence, He always finds a way for me to let go of the anger and find peace that surpasses all understanding. In fact, this is the verse I held onto during that time:

Philippians 4:7
And the peace of God which transcends all understanding, will guard your heart and your mind in Christ Jesus.

And He continued speaking to my heart: *I have told you that life begins at conception* (Psalm 139:13-16). *I am not taking this little one away from you. I am only keeping him safely with me until the day you join us. I know you love children, especially babies, and now you know that when you leave this world there will be one awaiting you.*

The mental picture of Jesus holding my baby in one arm and extending the other arm to hold me, was breathtaking. I will carry it with me throughout my life. How fortunate that I spewed all this out on the Lord and not my husband. There was not a man in the world that could give me the kind of peace that I was now feeling. Many of us rely on our spouse for a level of comfort and understanding that is not always humanly possible to give.

Now, back to my more recent miscarriage and my husband who, this time around, is not at peace. This pregnancy made it much easier to see, feel, and know the reality of a baby. In fact, the only reason I could be so strong was because God and I had already "gone there" together during the last miscarriage. I was sad, but not angry. I knew God would be faithful despite my lack of understanding. But my husband was struggling to get there. Oh how I wanted to be the one to make it all better for him, but from experience, I knew there was only One with that kind of power - and it wasn't me. So I left that morning for my Bible study, with my husband's question heavy on my heart. When I arrived, every woman in the room stood up, lined up, and hugged me. They weren't ignoring the pain, they were literally embracing it with me. It was just what my heart needed. As our prayer chairman, Karen, held me close she whispered in my ear, "God must really trust you, to allow you to go through this." It was as if God had handed me the answer to my husband's question on a silver platter. I continued to process this throughout the morning and when I got home I was bursting to tell him what was given to me. "When a teenager or a drug addict lose a baby, their reaction is probably one of relief, assuming they didn't want to be pregnant to begin with," I said. "Typically, the life of a little one born into the world under difficult circumstances isn't fully valued until much later (as every talent based television show will attest to during their back-story-segment). But when we lost our baby at just 13 weeks, that's a loss of great value - now! It's a life that won't ever be forgotten and best of all: a life that God can use right away. We have seen and delivered a child in such a rare and unusual way. God has been right by our side the whole time. Reaching down into the toilet, photographing the fetus in my hand, writing a letter to the baby only hours after his death...who does that? Looking back, I gave no thought to any of those things - I just did them. Being so 'in the moment' with such careful documentation, is not a human response to tragedy. God must really trust us."

The next day, our family planted a rose bush that had been given to us by my friend Amanda, as a beautiful outward reminder of a life that is now living in eternity. To my surprise, my husband took charge in digging the hole, placing our wrapped baby beneath, and over time tending to the care of this plant. Later, he would ask me if I noticed all the new buds that were visible.

I get it now: he cares for this plant because he can. If this baby had been born in our timing, my husband would have actively cared for him, and in a short time been able to bond with him. As women, it's easy to take for granted the bond we quickly make with our developing baby. Often, by the time a baby is born, the mom has already been caring and bonding with her lifeline attachment for nine months, while dads are just now getting their first direct opportunity.

Healing comes in all forms and at no set time. As individuals, we heal differently. My healing started with a temper tantrum towards God. My husband's healing involved far fewer words, as he cared and tended to that rose bush. How special it is to be loved by a God that knows you so intimately. He patiently listens to our angry, hurting hearts and then reaches out and heals us in a way that is completely unique to the person He created us to be.

Habakkuk 1:2,5

How long, O Lord, must I call for help, but you do not listen?

Or cry out to you, "Violence!" but you do not save?

(The Lord answers)

"Look at the Nations and watch – and be utterly amazed. For I am

going to do something in your days that you would not believe,

even if you were told."

HAPPY FATHER-FILLED DAY

Zephaniah is a collection of poetry that addresses God's once good and perfect world from Genesis now completely turned around. It states that it is not God's intention to bring destruction with fire of judgment, but rather purification. The goal being to **transform the hearts of nations into one family that collectively calls on the Name of the Lord.** Zephaniah depicts the people in the city of Jerusalem singing and rejoicing alongside the Lord, who also celebrates with songs of joy.

I woke up alone, on an overcast June morning in a beautiful two-bedroom villa in Newport, California. When I booked my timeshare week the previous summer, I didn't think to remember that the third Sunday in June was Father's Day. It was the first Father's Day without my own dad and the fourth Father's Day without my kids who were spending it with their dad. It had been an emotional week, watching fellow vacationers celebrate the wonderful men in their life. It was bittersweet for me to reflect back on my own special memories over the years. Coming to this timeshare as a blissful family-of-four had become a 10-year tradition. Three of those years, we brought my parents with us. My sister's family already lived in Orange County, so they would join us for a few days as well. Oh, how my dad loved swimming with his grandchildren in the giant hotel pool and enjoying a week entirely focused on his beautiful legacy. It really was the best! I will always cherish those amazing summer moments, like Mom in her wheelchair enjoying the

villa activities with cool ocean breezes on a body that tends to get overheated as a result of her MS. Without the physical strength of a man though, it will be tough to bring her here again - that is if she would even feel comfortable coming back without my dad.

So there I was, ready to check out of the hotel. It had been a nice week overall. My boys were there for the first part, until they had to leave to spend the holiday weekend at their dad's. The days on my own, I met up with some local friends, managed to get a perfect golden tan, and was two chapters shy of finishing a good read, poolside. As I loaded my luggage in the car, I remembered there was a Christian

Pool Games
11-12pm

mega church just down the street. I had always been curious about it, so I decided to pop in for Sunday service on my way home. Upon pulling into the parking lot, I was quickly reminded again of what day it was. There were signs everywhere welcoming dads to church. Greeters staggered around the campus voicing well wishes to each fatherly type who walked by. Ugh! This was already a bad idea.

I found a comfortable seat off to the side of the immense sanctuary where I could somewhat isolate and not stick out like a lonely sore thumb. The church was huge! I couldn't imagine they would fill all these seats, but they nearly did. Sitting there quietly, I remembered a statistic I once heard from a pastor, years ago:

While Mother's Day is a highly attended church day, Father's Day typically has the lowest church attendance. That's because on Mother's Day, men who don't typically attend church, will. They come with their wives or mothers to accompany and honor the special Mom in their life. But on Father's Day, many single women who do attend church regularly, opt not to. The reminder of being without a dad or without a husband, as you listen to a sermon on God's calling to men, is just too difficult. I never clearly understood that explanation... until that very moment.

I cried a bit during the worship songs, but oddly enough that always makes me feel better. I used to be uncomfortable raising my hands when singing in church. In all honesty, I often judged those around me who did. To me it seemed a bit showy or weird. But then one Sunday, while volunteering in childcare, my perspective changed. I spent most of the hour trying to console a little girl who wanted her daddy. At one point, she was so upset that we actually needed to page her dad out of the church service to come get her. When he walked in the room, her face lit up and her arms shot up to be held by him. It moved me to see how his presence instantly comforted her. Now, whenever I'm singing in church and I feel the Lord's presence before me, I tear up and have this strong desire to lift my arms, so my Father can comfort me. I'm sure there are people looking at me, like I used to look at others. But in that moment, just like that two-year-old little girl, there is only One I'm thinking about.

After singing, we were invited to greet one another. I was pleasantly surprised how many people approached me and genuinely welcomed me into their big church family. The pastor took centerstage and I felt my heart quickly building an armored wall. I anticipated his sermon would start with a shout out to all the strong, committed dads who came to church today. I was sure the role of a Father and how vital he is for the health of the family would be the pastor's main topic. Again, what was I thinking visiting here on this Sunday, of all Sundays?

You can imagine my surprise, when he started his sermon this way...

Before I get into today's message, I'd like to honor all the single mothers out there (a collective applause echoed through the massive church). I know that your job can't be easy. But I want you to know that when you parent your kids without their dad by your side, God will equip you. You have a Heavenly Father, who will never leave you or forsake you. He, himself, will be your helpmate when raising your children. God is also Father to the fatherless. When you think you are alone, be confident in knowing you have a Heavenly Father who loves you and is just waiting for you to let Him fill that void. Bless you beautiful daughters of the Almighty King.

Why is God always so kind to me? The remainder of the pastor's message was what one might expect to hear on this day set aside to honor dads. But now, my armor was off and I was in a place to receive it.

I am not without a Father. I am no longer burdened by the thought of forever spending this day alone. My eyes have been opened and my heart has been restored, once again.

Zephaniah 3: 16-17, 20

On that day they will say to Jerusalem, "Do not fear, O Zion; do not let your hands hang limp. The Lord your God is with you, He is mighty to save. He will take great delight in you, He will quiet you with his love, He will rejoice over you with singing."

I will give you honor and praise among all the peoples of the earth when I restore your fortunes before your very eyes," says the Lord.

A GLORIOUS TEMPLE

As the people of Jerusalem continue to rebuild the city, Haggai accuses them of not having their priorities in order. Collectively, they are focusing their time on building their own houses instead of building the temple. A warning is given that **obedience leads to blessings and unfaithfulness leads to ruins**. The Book of Haggai ends with the hope of a bright future hanging in the balance.

....

The first few months in our new Ventura County home, I was focused on making things just right for Mom and me. I had a wonderful friend who came alongside this DIY daughter of a carpenter, to reconstruct my mom's bathroom to accommodate her wheelchair more easily. Together with a hired contractor, in just two weeks time, we widened the doorway, lowered the sink, and took down a wall to make the closet and the bathroom one large area where Mom could easily maneuver. This must-do-project led to other less imperative projects, involving painting, decorating, purchasing household items, and planting

trees and shrubs. All of which proved productive, but quite time-consuming. In fact, so time-consuming that weekend after weekend I skipped out on going to the House of the Lord and directed my attention to the house of Preston.

While our home itself became more functional and appealing, my disposition did not. Have you ever felt so out of sorts that you can't even stand to be around yourself? It sounds strange, but that's exactly how I felt. I was working so hard to make this house our home, I lost touch with the house that keeps me grounded and connected – God's House. After months of being "too busy for church," I was parched, dehydrated, and in desperate need of something to quench my thirst.

Less than two miles from our new home was a quaint, non-denominational Christian Church that welcomed me in, and within only a matter of weeks, I had a whole new community of friends that felt like family.

I remember the first time I sat in the church's sanctuary. I instantly noticed the two wooden panels on each side of the stage that lit up with the words: "LOVE GOD" and "LOVE NEIGHBORS." It's such a simple concept that literally encompasses everything. The second Sunday I walked into the church, I was shocked when the

pastor remembered my name after just meeting me one week before. That same morning, I noticed a few announcements in their bulletin that caught my eye. The first one was that Community Bible Study was being held at their church on Wednesday mornings. I used to attend CBS when I lived in the San Fernando Valley, so I definitely wanted to check into attending again. The next announcement was the need for more children's leaders during Sunday morning services. Children are therapy for me, so I made sure to grab a volunteer application on the way out. Lastly, there was a class called Wholyfit that met on the church campus on Monday nights. An exercise class without judgment? Sign me up for that! Wow, I had a busy week ahead of me. I inwardly made a pact with the Lord: As long as it doesn't interfere with my ability to care for my mom, I will keep an open mind about every invitation You send me.

First up was Wholyfit. The Pilates-style stretch class not only gave me relief from lifting my mom throughout the day but also was filled with worship songs and Bible verses of encouragement. I met a handful of friendly women from the church and one of them invited me to the small group Bible study she attends on Wednesday nights. So two nights later, after getting Mom situated in her recliner, I drove down the street to join my new friend, Debbie, at her neighborhood small group. I prayed silently as I drove, that perhaps one day I would be entrusted to host a small group study in the convenience of our handicapped-accessible home so that my mom might attend too.

When I arrived, there were about 12 people in the group; some older, some younger, some married, some single, some new to reading the Bible, some quite knowledgeable about Scripture. While we all appear to be a bunch of "randoms," we all have the only thing we need in common: the desire to learn, share, and grow in Jesus. As we gathered together in a large, seated circle in the host's living room, I realized this was the home of the pastor and his wife, and he was the leader of this group. In all the years I'd been a part of mid-week Bible studies, I had never had the honor of discussing last week's sermon with the man who actually gave it, and never would I imagine doing this from inside his home.

The hour-long discussion flew by and I really enjoyed everyone's insights. There was this spunky, fun-loving, 92-year-old woman named Phyllis sitting across from me. Oh how I wish my mom could have met her. They truly would have hit it off. Just before we closed the night in prayer, Pastor Bruce announced that he and his wife enjoy leading the group, but would like to take a break from hosting and offer another member the opportunity. He asked that each of us pray about it and discuss it with our households and email him during the week if anyone is interested.

As much as I wanted to shoot my hand straight into the air, I humbly recalled that I was brand new to this church and they may be more comfortable with a member who didn't just start coming a week and a half ago. Plus, maybe there were people who had been in this group for years and had been patiently waiting for an opportunity to host.

Perhaps it was my reward for biting my tongue and waiting on the Lord. But it turned out that no one volunteered to host and when I sent an email to Pastor Bruce the second week, he was delighted. We took a short Summer break and when the neighborhood groups started back up in August, Mom and I got to open our beautiful new home to a beautiful new group of friends. And Mom and Phyllis became as thick as thieves.

Within a few weeks of being cleared as a Children's Volunteer, I was asked to be the lead teacher for their classroom in greatest need: Pre-Kindergarten. How was this amazing stage at 4 and 5 years-old left just for me? It was so nice to be back with "my people" again.

I was a little apprehensive about spending more time away from Mom by possibly joining the Wednesday morning Community Bible Study, until one of the ladies there told me about the city's shuttle system. It provides complete wheelchair access with ramps and drivers who handle everything. You schedule a pick-up from your house and they drop you off at the door of wherever you are going within the city limits. My mom could get the senior citizen

rate of $1.50 per ride, and I could travel with her for free as her caregiver. I loved the idea of Mom getting out of the house at least one day a week, meeting new friends, and stretching herself a little; all for the bargain price of $3. Now I just need to get her to agree to it.

It's not that my mom would be opposed to studying the Bible. She has always been a believer, but was raised to go to church in her Sunday best and keep her beliefs quietly to herself the rest of the week. Since being in a wheelchair, I've only gotten her to go to church when my boys are home for Christmas and Easter. Getting her in and out of a car is awkward and requires fully lifting her in and out of her wheelchair. Since my dad's passing, she doesn't want to leave the house unless she has to see a doctor, or for a truly special occasion. But now that we've moved to a new home in a new community, I'm hoping for a new open mind. "Mom, I'd like you to try it one time. If you absolutely don't want to go back the following week, I won't force it," I bargained. I could have sworn I had this exact conversation in reverse with her 40-something years ago when she wanted to sign me up for ballet and tap. Anyway, she agreed and although this was completely out of her comfort zone, she didn't hate it.

That week we answered the questions out of our lesson books together and for this being her first in-depth Bible study, she did quite well. She didn't have a lot of answers, but she did have a willing heart and an open mind. I just hoped that positive attitude would carry over into traveling back on the shuttle next Wednesday. The day before, I reminded her we would need to call the service and reserve our ride if she wanted to attend. She thought for a minute, and then said, "Well I don't want any of those ladies to think I didn't do my homework, so I guess I better go."

Now, a year and a half later, she is known as "Little Miss Sunshine" to the leaders and other women attending the study. She is quite eager to answer the questions each week and has proved to be one of the more vocal women in her group. Since transitioning to Zoom for both our Bible studies, she now just wheels up beside me and spreads her sunshine through the digital platform.

On Sunday mornings she listens-in from her room as I teach a Zoom Pre-K Sunday school class. She is always inspired by the kid's pure love for the Lord and enjoys hearing the sound of children's voices ringing in our home. What a blessing to bring God's house to our house.

Haggai 2:9
"The glory of this present house will be greater than the glory of the former house. And in this place I will grant peace," declares the Lord Almighty.

A NEW GENERATION

In the Book of Zechariah there is a challenge given to the Israelites who are still in exile: **Turn back to the Lord and move away from your ancestors way of thinking** - refusing to listen and rebelling in their own selfishness. Zechariah has a number of odd dreams that look to a future world filled with peace. This new generation of Israelites is about to be released out of exile and expected to rise above the chaos that will ensue as they **hope for the promise of a peaceful future.**

....

At the age of eight, Ryan was cast in a recurring role on a network series. Upon arriving to set the first day, we met the studio teacher as she was assisting a little girl, also cast as a series regular on the show. I remembered this little actress from the audition process. More so, I remembered sitting with her mom in the casting office waiting area a few times. She stood out to me because I was curious about their family dynamic. Both the young actress and her mom had light skin and very much resembled each other, but the woman's younger daughter in tow was of mixed-race. There wasn't much for a "momager" to do while waiting in a casting office for the powers that be to finish with your kid, so I came up with some scenarios in my head to explain my confusion: the younger daughter perhaps was adopted, or came from a second marriage, or innocently called her babysitter "Mom." But that day, I would learn that I was wrong on all three of my assumptions. Because right after the studio teacher introduced us to Ryan's castmate Paige, two women walked in the door behind us. The teacher then said, "Oh and this is Paige's mom and Paige's other mom." I recognized the shorter woman from the auditions, but the six-foot tall African American woman caught me off guard. We smiled and shook each other's hands, as I now performed in my own acting role of "one who is perfectly comfortable in this situation." I so wanted to embrace this fourth scenario of a bi-racial, two-mom family dynamic – but it was hard for me. Ryan on the other hand, put aside his acting skills and just embraced the situation as he often does as different and perfectly okay. Having recently had the "egg and sperm talk," he later had a few questions for me on the mechanics of how two moms can birth a child, but after a brief lesson on insemination, he was as accepting as always. I sometimes wondered if I was telling Ryan too much at such a young age, but he was relentlessly inquisitive. So rather than make stuff up, I went with the truth, and surprisingly he did well with that. It made me wonder if I would have had more of an open mind as an adult if some truths of this world were given to me while I was still young and not so set on things in my mind.

In the weeks and months to follow, we grew to know our stage family quite well. Both Ryan and Paige were each in a few scenes every week during the eight months it took to film Season One. They were also the only two children who were cast on the show, so we spent eight-hour days on set together a few days each week. To keep myself busy, I would often bring my Bible study homework to work on while Ryan was in studio school. I suppose I was just as comfortable displaying my identity in Christ, as the other moms were in displaying their identity in what brought them joy. I think authenticity is such an attractive quality, regardless if I'm in agreement or not with what honest attribute is being expressed. I knew that bringing my Bible to a Hollywood studio opens myself up to judgment, but so be it. Just like Paige's moms, my intent was in no way to make others feel uncomfortable or to create division. On the contrary, I welcomed anyone who would like to discuss or even question my belief. Not in a harsh, intolerant sort of way, but as one truly seeking to understand another's view; I suppose like Jesus Himself did when He encountered people of all types along His path.

Paige's mom, Sonya, was the fellow stage mom I spent my long days on set with. At times, the topic of me expressing my faith and her expressing her identity came up in a respectful and inquisitive manner. We heard what each other had to say and even asked questions openly.

I remember she told me that when she was a teenager, she had such a crush on the lead actor who was playing the role of Paige's dad on the show. I was so confused. I thought the general rule was that one was "born gay." I then recalled having girl crushes on Wonder Woman and Heather Locklear growing up, so my confusion soon dissipated.

What's interesting was that I sometimes wondered, "Did I choose God or did God choose me?" Closeness with the Lord is something I had felt from a very young age, more so than the rest of my family. Even when I questioned God's existence in tough times - I couldn't deny His presence in all aspects of my life from as far back as I could remember. While I knew that inevitably we all have free will and make our own choices, I truly felt like the desire to fully love God was something I was born with. So while Christianity was my choice, it was an easy one for me.

Sonya and I agreed that some concepts can't be easily simplified, and even if they could, it wouldn't make a difference in the outcome. Throughout our time together, Sonya didn't personally feel drawn towards Christianity anymore than I personally felt drawn towards homosexuality. They were identities we felt strongly about in our own lives, and we learned that we could have a very enjoyable friendship because there were so many other ways we could relate to each other.

Sadly, the show did not get picked up for a second season, so our time together came to an end. We have kept up on Facebook and while our political and religious views may differ, our care for one another does not. Later on, I remember running into Paige and both of her moms at a commercial audition. It had been years since we'd all seen each other. The large casting office was packed with kids and parents. (Typically there is not much "fraternizing with the enemy" to be seen, as everyone around you is your competition.) But when Ryan's eyes met Paige's, they both left their mothers' sides and ran to embrace like long lost friends. We all gathered in a big teary hug in the middle of the crowded waiting area. I recognized some confused stares from the outside of our unconventional huddle, but I didn't care. There is a difference in seeing with your eyes and seeing with your heart. I was proud of our genuine love for each other and so grateful to have broken free from my old ways of avoiding those who were different from me. My heart had been restored to the way God created it to be.

Zechariah 7:9-10
This is what the Lord Almighty says: Administer true justice; show mercy and compassion to one another. Do not oppress the widow or the fatherless, the alien or the poor. In your hearts do not think evil of each other.

TRUST AND SEE

In the Book of Malachi we see a new generation of Israelites, who are like their ancestors; complaining of God neglecting them. Their selfishness is confronted as they are commanded to **turn back in faithfulness** by tithing (giving 1/10 of one's income to the House of the Lord). **God will bless those who are faithful to give of what they have to bless others.** Logically this made no sense to the people and many neglected their tithe. A Scroll of Remembrance, pointing them to God's character of the past is given to inspire hope for the future. In the end, it is not earthly riches God desires from us - but a trusting relationship with Him.

When I began teaching Kindergarten at West Valley Christian Academy (WVCA), I had the privilege of teaching at the very same school that my children attended. In fact, I was blessed to have each of my sons in my Kindergarten class (2003 and 2005). But the year in between these two experiences was also very special to me.

As a staff member of this small private school (often referred to as "the best kept secret in the valley"), I was given 50% off of tuition for my children each year. What a deal! I get paid for spending the whole day with my boys and their friends, and then only pay half as much as other parents do who must drop their kids off. I knew I was blessed and I thanked God everyday for it. In 2004 there was a sweet family at our church who were loved by all. Chad played keyboard for the worship team and Kelly was a stay-home-mom to two of the cutest little girls I've ever known. Money was tight, but they were resourceful as they took on the role of apartment managers to help offset their rent and living expenses. It wasn't until their oldest daughter Mali was about to start Kindergarten that they really felt the sting of disappointment. Many of the families from our church sent their children to WVCA. Financially speaking, this was not feasible for Chad and Kelly. And unfortunately, the public school in their area was known for performing poorly academically, and of course would lack the biblical foundation they desired for their daughter to have.

Kelly looked into homeschooling, but managing an apartment and a three-year-old while trying to teach her Kindergartner to read and write, seemed unimaginable.

When friends would chat after church about their kids and ask one another about plans for the upcoming school year, Chad and Kelly would often say, "We are praying for God to make a way." Other people began to pray too, asking God to please create a way for little Mali to attend Kindergarten at WVCA with her friends and Jesus. By now, you may have guessed where this story is going. Yes, God put it on my heart to use the very tuition amount I was excused from paying and give it to this family for Mali to attend. At the risk of sounding boastful, I have to admit this was an easy decision for me. In fact, I couldn't wait to put God's plan in motion. There was just one hurdle I'd have to get past... getting my husband to agree to it. Having had many long discussions with differing opinions on giving and tithing, this was one topic I often actively avoided. But each time I would pray, I felt God strongly telling me, "I've already given you the answer to this prayer, as well as the means to follow through. Why do you keep asking me?" So I approached my husband with a humble spirit, and an open mind.

I was prepared for a "Why us? There are other people at church who drive nicer cars and live in bigger houses. Why should we be the ones to step up and help?"

But to my surprise, that was not at all his reaction. His response was, "I don't feel the same tug, but if it's really what you think God is calling you to do, then let's do it." I seized the opportunity of the moment to clarify that I wanted this to be a gift offering, separate from our weekly tithe to the church. He understood and agreed. It was as if God had gone before me and softened his heart towards my humble request.

I also recalled that just one year before, we had experienced God's hand upon our tithing in a memorable way. As members and regular attenders at our church, we decided to conveniently tithe online, giving a set amount each week. My husband's job was based solely on commission, so this option made giving a tenth of our income rather inaccurate. But we agreed on a conservative amount and that was that. After a surprisingly good year, my husband ended up losing a steady client company. This made his income for the following year drop in such a way that the set amount we were tithing now truly became an accurate tenth of our income. Some may say that's a weird coincidence, but for me it was a powerful lesson. It was as if God was saying, "If this is the amount you want to give, then this is the amount you'll need to make." Perhaps this recent lesson in obedience was impacting my husband's heart in this new giving opportunity, but I didn't ask.

Regardless of the reasoning, I wasted no time in calling Kelly and asking her if she would allow us to be used by God to come alongside her family in answering this prayer. She was grateful and speechless. My only condition was that she not tell anyone that the funds came from us. She tearfully agreed, and just a few weeks before school started, Mali was enrolled in WVCA. I am only now (with Kelly's permission) sharing this "nice thing" I did because it pales in comparison with the flood of blessings that God had in store for all of us. It didn't take long for good news to travel around to our friends at church. When I first heard, "Did you hear God provided a way for Mali to go to WVCA?", my heart leapt from inside. To be the secret agent in God's under-cover-covering operation was one of the greatest honors ever given to me. Another blessing I wasn't prepared for was that I would be assigned to be Mali's Kindergarten teacher. To have a front-row seat to watch God's plan unfold in this little girl still brings tears to my eyes.

Mali's thirst for learning was nothing like I'd ever seen. She asked to borrow a different book from our classroom library everyday before going home. She wanted more than anything to learn to read. She walked into Kindergarten barely knowing the sounds of each letter of the alphabet but ended the year in the top reading group. She visibly loved learning and she was never absent or tardy.

A couple times during the year, I would open my classroom door at 3 p.m. to find Kelly standing outside with a large bag that held a home-cooked meal for me to enjoy with my family that night. She would pick her daughter up from school and say, "I know when you leave here, you have papers to grade and a young family of your own to care for, so I made extra. I hope this blesses you." (And it greatly did!)

As if those heartfelt blessings weren't enough of a "return on my investment," God did something in the spring of that year that was *Awe-mazing*! Not only were we able to sell our home and move to a larger home in a better neighborhood, but our house sold for $10,000 **over** asking price. This was exactly double the $5,000 tuition we gifted Mali. This is why I feel zero arrogance in telling you this story. God will out-give you every time, if you let him.

God blesses obedience. We obeyed God's calling to give, and Chad and Kelly obeyed God in taking their request not only to Him, but allowing others to seek the Lord whole-heartedly on their behalf. In the end, all of our hearts were filled beyond measure. Mali thrived, our financial gift was returned to us far more than twofold, and God got all the glory!

Trust Him, Obey Him, and let Him surprise you abundantly.

Malachi 3:10

"Bring the whole tithe into the storehouse, that there may be food in my house. Test me in this," says the LORD Almighty, "and see if I will not throw open the floodgates of Heaven and pour out so much blessing that there will not be room enough to store it."

Update:

The following year Chad and Kelly moved their family to Texas. Mali continued to soar academically. In May of 2020 she graduated from college Magna Cum Laude and now works on staff at the very church this whole God moment started from. And I'm excited to attend her wedding in June 2021.

WHY PRAY?

Matthew is the first book of the New Testament and the first book of the Bible where we meet Jesus in the flesh. Jesus clearly states that He is not here to set aside the teachings of the Old Testament, but to fulfill them. **Jesus desires to transform hearts so that people can truly love God, love their neighbors, and even love their enemies.** Jesus introduces us to God as a loving Father who wants a real relationship with all of His children.

....

I used to struggle with the concept of prayer. I mean why would an all-powerful God want me interjecting my ideas on how I think things should go? Can I change His mind? If I believe He's "all knowing," shouldn't I just trust His decisions, without voicing my own opinions on the matter? Furthermore, if He truly knows my heart, He already knows that I love Him. Why even express myself to Him?

Whenever I don't get God, it always helps me to view him through the lens of a parent. Whether you are a parent yourself or have only experienced parenting through the people who raised you – everybody on Earth can relate to what parenting looks like. What if children never told their parents that they loved them? What if they never shared their hopes and dreams or disappointments with Mom or Dad? Truthfully, nobody has to listen to their kids - a parent makes the final decision. Additionally, a child's actions should show that they love their parent, so why bother saying it? (Ouch! That sentence hurt to write.) A relationship with the Lord becomes clear when I think of God as my parent. Without truly expressing to Him how I feel or what I fear or what my heart desires, it's impossible to have a meaningful relationship. Just as we want to hear from our children, God does too. He wants to comfort us, bless us, love us, and even discipline us for our greater good. When we communicate with Him, we open our hearts and minds to all He has to show us and give us.

In Matthew 5, Jesus began His first sermon to the people who were following Him. During His precious time in Galilee, He taught the people how to pray. I found it helpful to use the letters P-R-A-Y to guide me through my own personal prayer, based on the one that Jesus modeled for us:

Praise – You are my protector, my healer, my comforter, and the light on my path. I not only thank You for the life, people, and things You have given me; but also for the ability to come to You whenever and wherever I want. Thank You for Your unending faithfulness in my life. (Our Father, who art in Heaven, hallowed be Your name)

Repent – I'm sorry for the times I've put my ways and desires above what You have for me. I want to not only forgive others, but also to forgive myself for the times I've fallen short. Help me to forgive like You do, Lord. (Forgive us our debts, as we also have forgiven our debtors)

Ask – Please give me what I need and please consider what I want. May I have Your wisdom in making hard choices and may I walk in a way that honors You. Please protect me from being tempted down paths that are not of You. (Give us today our daily bread. Lead us not into temptation, but deliver us from the evil one)

Yield – What I'm asking might not be what is best for me right now, but You know. Your heavenly perspective allows You to see the big picture. I understand that I can only see what's right in front of me. I trust that if You don't give this to me, You can change my heart to no longer want it, or to wait for it in Your perfect timing (Your Kingdom come, Your will be done, on Earth as it is in Heaven)

In the name of Jesus, who taught us to pray; **AMEN**

In John 16:23, we are told that the Father will give you whatever you ask in My name. I don't always receive what I ask for, but I know that God has heard and received my prayer. He will give me what is best, as praying in the name of Jesus shows that I am surrendering to His will. I also pray "in Jesus' name," as it makes it clear to anyone listening or joining me in prayer, exactly which God I am praying to. Many people will pray to God, but not all believe in Jesus Christ as His Son. To me, a God that is not the Father of Jesus is not the same God.

There is a popular expression that says, "Be careful what you pray for." This phrase is meant as a clever warning that God may actually give you exactly what you ask for. Back when I was first invited to go to Africa on a mission trip, I got myself out of the conversation by saying, "I'll pray about it and see how God leads." The next week during West Valley Christian Academy's teacher's meeting, we were asked by the principal if there were any prayer requests. I decided to share with my coworkers the opportunity I was given to go on a teaching mission trip to Uganda over the summer. Looking back, I thought if I passed the buck on to someone else to pray, then I could check it off my list and not actually deal with making a decision. What I hadn't considered is that the group of teachers I asked to pray actually would, and that God would actually answer them.

Over the next month I had three different women approach me privately and tell me in their own way that they'd been praying and really felt God's hand in this opportunity - I should go. I began to make excuses about how expensive it was and that while my husband worked from home, I couldn't expect him to watch and entertain our active boys for two weeks. But these wise, prayerful fellow teachers encouraged me to keep an open mind and keep praying about it. Now that God truly had my attention, He wasted no time easing my doubts and giving me clarity.

In lieu of an end-of-the-year teacher's gift, my Kindergarten Room Mom took up a collection towards my potential trip, which helped considerably in paying my airfare to Uganda. A couple of families from school graciously volunteered to have my boys over for play dates while I would be away. One family even invited my boys and their dad on a house boating vacation for five days during my 14 day trip. The school I worked at donated books and teaching supplies for me to gift the teachers in Uganda. When I said, "I'll see how God leads," I most certainly did.

As you may have already read – I did go. I have more to tell you about that first trip in the story from Ephesians. But I will tell you now that it was one of the best experiences of my life. Because I prayed and asked others to pray too, I went in full confidence, knowing that this was God's will for me. He not only was going to bless this experience, but He would be right there beside me throughout it.

Matthew 6:9-13

"This then is how you should pray: Our Father in Heaven, hallowed be your name, your Kingdom come, your will be done, on Earth as it is in Heaven. Give us today our daily bread. And forgive us our debts, as we also have forgiven our debtors. And lead us not into temptation, but deliver us from the evil one."

I'LL PRAY FOR YOU

In the Book of Mark, we see Jesus modeling prayer as He humbly asks His Father in the presence of His disciples, **"Abba, Father," He said, "everything is possible for You. Take this cup from me. Yet not what I will, but what You will" (Mark 14:36)**. There was only one way for God to fulfill Scripture and His promises, so He did not take that cup (the wrath of going to the cross) away from Jesus. But God did give His Son strength, wisdom, and peace in doing what needed to be done. By saying "no" to sparing Jesus' life, He would be able to say "yes" to saving all of ours through His Resurrection. Prayer is not always about what we can gain, it is also about trusting God in what we can give up.

> PRAYER IS NOT GETTING MAN'S WILL DONE IN HEAVEN, BUT GETTING GOD'S WILL DONE ON EARTH. IT IS NOT OVERCOMING GOD'S RELUCTANCE BUT LAYING HOLD OF GOD'S WILLINGNESS.
> RICHARD C. TRENCH

Often as a Christian, I am keenly aware that I don't have all the answers. But I know God does. When I hear of someone going through a hardship, illness, or time of uncertainty, I am quick to use the comforting phrase, "I'll pray for you." I am embarrassed to say that I have many times uttered these four well-intentioned words, then failed to follow through.

Having the words to pray isn't easy, and praying them out loud can be even harder. Despite this struggle, I try to step out of my comfort zone and pray for someone right there in the moment. Instead of proclaiming,

"I'll pray for you," I ask, "May I pray for you right now?" At first, I would just do this when I was physically with someone, like after church or walking with a friend. But I then realized I could also pray for others over the phone or in reply to a text. When friends on Facebook ask for prayer, I'll post a comment below that starts, "Lord, I lift up to you…" This outward expression of prayer made sense to me; why shouldn't we include others in our relationship with the Lord? I had watched fellow Christians pray out loud publicly with ease, and though it initially made me feel uneasy, I grew to desire to be more like them, caring enough to stop and go to God immediately.

A most memorable time of witnessing such prayer-filled boldness happened a few years back at lunch with my friend Michael.

After the waitress took our order, Michael asked, "Sophie," as stated on her nametag. "We're going to pray before our meal, and I just wondered if there is anything we could include in our prayer for you?"

His out-of-the-box question took me completely by surprise. Not only did *I* feel awkward myself, but I felt super uncomfortable for Sophie. She too was taken aback. But then there was this visible softening of her countenance.

"Actually, my mom is really sick. I'd love for you to pray for her," she shared.

Michael smiled kindly and said, "Of course. What's your mom's name?"

Suddenly, there was no more discomfort. In fact it was the exact opposite. I felt blessed to be part of this very unorthodox moment.

Sophie answered his question with a smile of gratitude and returned back to her waitressing responsibilities. As I joined Michael in a quiet yet audible prayer at our restaurant table, I peeked out from the corner of my eye to see Sophie looking back in humble disbelief. I'm sure, struck by the fact that a stranger would want to pray for her and her mom - and by name. Regardless of how God answers that prayer, there is a universal love that is felt by simply making His presence in our problems known. I was privileged to witness Michael do this a handful of times. He didn't take prayer requests every time we ate out, just the times he felt moved by the Holy Spirit to ask. In most cases, the servers were always thankful and often had a request to offer as a quick "shout up to God." I remember one waiter stating, "Nah, I'm all good." Michael's reply? "Awesome, we'll praise God for that!" And we did.

Praying for strangers is actually how I met my close friend, Carol. We didn't know anything about one another when we were placed in the same breakout group at Bible Study Fellowship. The BSF organization was focused on learning the Bible without sharing or discussing outside opinions or sources. We were encouraged to have our only source of information be God's Word and not share about specific churches, pastors, books, political news... you get the idea. Each week, our discussion group of 10 people would share our personal answers to the lesson's questions. Based on Carol's answers, I was able to decipher that she had two children the same ages as mine, and her oldest would be starting a new school in the fall. As a fellow busy mom who would be going back to teaching in the fall myself, I enjoyed hearing her share and often could relate to what she was saying. I appreciated her concerns as a parent and having to really rely on God when seeking right decisions for her children.

The study ended in May and I found myself thinking about and praying for Carol at various times over the summer. She was so anxious about choosing the right school for her children, I wish I could have comforted her as a knowing teacher and an understanding mom. I felt remiss that I hadn't gotten to know her better. Perhaps our five-year-olds and three-year-olds could have played together in the park while we simply chatted about life. Though I may have missed my opportunity to be able to contact her once the study was over, I could still take the opportunity to pray for her on her journey. God even gave me the perfect reminder. That June, when I got my class list of students' names, I noticed that I had a student named Paul. I remembered that was also her son's name, God's way of naturally bringing her to mind during my summer prep-time.

September came and as I welcomed the new families at our traditional "Meet and Greet" gathering, there was Carol standing in the center of my classroom. It took us a minute, but we then realized the reality of the situation. She came over and hugged me while saying, "I've been praying for Paul's new Kindergarten teacher all summer, but I had no idea I was praying for you!" With tears in our eyes we both gave a chuckle, recalling how funny God can sometimes be.

Paul and Blake, and Gracie and Ryan had many future play-dates together in parks, as well as plenty of other places. To this day, 17 years later, our children still keep in touch. Carol has become like a sister to me and has been a source of refuge during my toughest life battles. We have also had a lot of laughs too. One of my favorite questions to answer is, "How did you two become friends?"

"Well, basically, we prayed for each other."

Mark 14:32
They went to a place called Gethsemane, and Jesus said to His
disciples, "Sit here while I pray."

THANKS FOR THE BURNT BACON

Much like the other three gospels, the Book of Luke tells us of Jesus' many miracles. These miracles were performed so that people could see and believe that Jesus was the Son of God. Most of these miracles involved impossible healing transformations to the physical body. In turn, **hearts were also transformed through witnessing such a wondrous act of God's grace and mercy.**

....

I've always been big on thank you's. I guess it's just the way my parents raised me. But I do firmly believe that acknowledging someone's kindness towards you or appreciating another's positive impact on your world should never go unnoticed. I suppose I too was a stickler at this as a young mom, for I can remember being told what wonderful manners my little boys had. "Why, thank you!"

As one who elevates the virtue of gratitude, I struggled for years to understand the story of Jesus healing the 10 men with leprosy in the book of Luke. These 10 men stood at a distance, shouting and begging for Jesus to heal them. Jesus hears their plea and tells them:

Luke 17:14
"Go and show yourselves to the priests." And as they went they were cleansed.

All ten of these men were healed before they even got to where the priests were located. Jesus blessed them for simply being obedient.

But here is the part I've always struggled with: Only one of the men came back, thanking and praising God. Really?! Jesus completely heals you from a deadly, disgraceful, painful disease and you don't feel the need to say, "thank you"? That was hard for me to imagine …until recently.

A few months ago, I noticed my neighbors across the street put an old propane BBQ out on the curb. Having my younger son home from college due to COVID-19, I thought it might be a good "stay home" activity for us. He could be my sous-chef from time to time and grill things for me. (I hear it's like therapy for most men.) So I rolled the BBQ across the street and into my backyard. I detached my propane tank from the base of my outdoor heater (that I still think I'm one day going to actually use) and attached it to my new find. I fired her up. She works! After a good cleaning, I vowed to not let my propane tank go to waste in this new location.

That weekend, I petitioned Ryan to take a break from pandemic-binge-video-game-playing and BBQ for me. I seasoned steaks and he seemed to enjoy his time behind the grill. Just as he was about to turn the knobs off, I suggested he leave the flame going. I had a couple pieces of raw bacon to use up and thought it would be interesting to see how they would cook on a BBQ. I threw them on, closed the lid, and had the best of intentions to check back on them in two minutes.

Twelve hours later, I bolted awake from a deep sleep at 4 a.m., remembering the bacon on my lit grill. I raced downstairs and out the back sliding door. I used a rag to open the rusted metal hood and a mass of black smoke puffed out at me. Just above the glowing flame lie four small charred pieces that could no longer be identified as bacon. I gasped a sigh of relief that I caught my mistake before something disastrous happened. Despite smelling like a chimney sweep, I went back to bed and slept another three hours.

That afternoon I grabbed my laptop and Zoomed-in to my weekly women's Bible study. My friend Marsha told us how she just got off the phone with her friend, whose house caught on fire last night. The family had gotten a new stove and there was either something in the wiring or it wasn't installed properly and a fire started in their kitchen. She went on to say how thankful they were that no one was hurt and that half of the downstairs and all of the upstairs were spared. In that moment, it was like a veil was lifted from my eyes as I realized: I'm one of the nine lepers! There I sat, in my intact home, completely untouched by the threat of my negligence. The results could have been tragic. The old BBQ that I centered against the back wall, directly under our kitchen window, could have easily taken over our enclosed patio with its heat. While my son and I slept unaware upstairs, my handicapped mom would have been confined to her bed downstairs. Oh the loss that could have been endured.

Thank you Jesus for protecting our home and the precious lives that it holds within. I'm so sorry that it took the thankfulness of another, who suffered far more than I did, to realize how blessed I am. Please forgive me for taking Your love for me and my family for granted. Thank You that You never sleep or that our actions never go unnoticed by You.

During this 2020 Covid-19 Pandemic, we are all so quick to complain and wonder where God is and why He would allow this to happen. Meanwhile, He is right here watching over us. He has never once asked us to understand His ways, only to trust that He will not leave us nor forsake us.

I heard a quote once that said, "What if God only gave you today, what you remembered to thank Him for yesterday?" Thank you Lord for all the times You rescue and bless me, especially those times that I am unaware of Your saving power at work in my life. And thank You that the only consequence I endured from my recent negligence was a couple of pieces of burnt bacon. Amen.

Luke 17:17-19

Jesus asked, "Were not all ten cleansed? Where are the other nine? Has no one returned to give praise to God except this foreigner? Then He said to him, Rise and go; your faith has made you well.

MADE KNOWN

In the Book of John, Jesus continues to help us understand God the Father: **To know Jesus is to know the Father.** Jesus spoke of His Father in Heaven in such a way, that whoever heard His words began to know God on a more intimate and personal level. Jesus reminds followers that they too can become **children of God and fellow heirs to the Kingdom.**

....

How many 83-year-old men do you know who do their own taxes after mowing their lawn? Then accomplishing the cooking, cleaning, and shopping before going to the gym and considering it all just in a day's work? Well, if you do, then you must know Big Al. Most people call him "amazing," but I am privileged to call him "Dad!" One of my favorite verses in the Bible is **John 14:2** where Jesus states, **My Father's house has many rooms: if that were not so, would I have told you that I am going there to prepare a place for you?**

As the child of a master carpenter who worked at the Beverly Hills Hotel for over 30 years, this was never a difficult piece of Scripture to grasp. I assumed everybody's daddy built their house, then built the furniture to go inside, and because daddies love their little girls so much, they design and construct two-story playhouses for the backyard. *Oh, wait - not all daddies do that?*

I soon learned my dad was not one in a million, but he was one of a kind! He gave graciously to those he called his own. His time, talk, and talents were valuable resources to our family. My dad became the hands and feet my mom needed on a daily basis when her disability became too great. He never took a sick day or left her side longer than a few hours. Providing 100% care for his lovely bride, he was my picture of dedication. He rarely went to church and I don't have memories of him reading the Bible, but he knew what it meant to *love like Jesus.*

Thankfully, my dad cared for himself, too. He worked out at the gym faithfully three times a week, every week, for 56 years! This is not an exaggerated truth. Growing up, I knew that if an event fell on a Monday, Wednesday, or Friday night it would have to be a major one if I expected my dad to attend. Those were his gym nights: 7 p.m. to 9 p.m. It was the one area he gave to himself and we all understood and supported the importance in keeping that time sacred. In fact, it was so sacred that I recall my mom once saying to me, "Thank God your sister was born on a Thursday."

Growing up, I thought it was cool to have a dad who always went to the gym. But what was even *cooler* was that he worked out at the Hollywood YMCA. In my young mind, this practically made him a movie star. Why Hollywood? Well that's the gym that was near his apartment when he became a member back in his twenties. He made friends there, he liked it there, so he stayed there. After a while, they stopped charging him a membership fee and gave him a sleeveless shirt that read "Instructor." I know, seriously the coolest guy ever! Up until the day he passed, he still worked out at this iconic location.

A few years ago, my son Ryan and I were driving home from a commercial audition in Hollywood. Ryan said, "Hey it's Friday. Let's skip the traffic and go visit Papa at the gym." Oh my! In all my life, I never once thought of actually going there. But then again, never did I think I would move back under my parents' roof with my two teenaged sons, but I did, just weeks before. (And if Dad could survive that shock with such grace and understanding, he most likely would come through with flying colors on this one too.) The young guy at the sign-in desk had never heard of Al Preston. Ryan and I stood motionless, both secretly wondering if we were in the right place. The complete shock on our

faces must have jarred this new employee a bit, for he encouraged us to walk around freely to look for him. My 14-year-old testosterone-driven son instinctively led us through meandering staircases and hallways until we arrived in the Weight Room. While I

knew my dad might very well have a heart attack after seeing us there on his sacred ground, I figured in the end that's probably how he would prefer to go. Thankfully, it was a pleasant surprise and I'm not sure who was more proud - my son seeing his pumped-up grandfather in action, or my dad introducing his strong, young grandson around to his gym-mates. This trip was well worth the dot on our unpredictable timeline of life's significant events.

Just a few months before my dad left this world, he came home from Big 5 with "skater shoes." When I saw them sitting in the living room,

I felt irritated as I wondered which one of my boys left for their dad's house and didn't put their shoes away. The next time I saw those shoes, they were attached to my dad's feet as he was walking out to go to the gym. He even got  compliments on them from the young guys in the Weight Room. He said he really only got them because they were soft and flexible, as well as on sale (of course). Well Dad, one thing's for certain... nobody could fill those shoes like you did. You are loved from the top of your beautiful bald head to the tip of your stylish feet!

Despite no longer having Dad here with me, talking about him brings me joy and such gratitude; gratitude for being blessed with such a wonderful man to call my own and gratitude that I will be with him again one day in Heaven. Even those who have never met him probably get a good sense of who he was and what he was like, just by my stories and heartfelt descriptions. Wanting to tell people about my earthly father and how he lived and loved so sacrificially - that comes easy to me. I'm now striving to share more about my Heavenly Father with even more pride and ease. It's Real to Me is a big part of how I hope to make Him more known to others.

John 1:18

No one has ever seen God, but the one and only Son, who
is Himself God and is in closest relationship with the Father,
has made Him known.

EVANGELIST: AGE 6

The Acts of the Apostles was written by Luke and is the book of the
Bible where Jesus' direct influence on the world ends and His faithful
disciples take over aided by the Spirit of God. Just before Jesus is
taken up to Heaven before the very eyes of His disciples, He has one
last important message for them. Jesus reminds them of the gift that
the Father has promised them: **One who will help them go out into
the world and be witnesses to all that has happened and all that
is still yet to come.**

....

The only thing that Ryan wanted for his sixth birthday was acting
classes. A few weeks before, he had watched his favorite Sunday
school teacher, Mr. Dave perform in a church play. Ryan was enamored
with Mr. Dave's role as an old, grouchy man. This character was nothing
like the cool, funny Sunday School teacher he'd grown to know and
love. The idea of pretending to be someone you're not fascinated Ryan
and he wanted in. So when he handed me his birthday wishlist with only
one thing on it, I knew he was serious.

As kids, my sister and I wanted to be television actresses, so our mom
indulged us and signed us up to work as "extras" for the studios. It
was awful. I would have to wake up before the sun was out, be driven
a million miles away, do busy work in a stuffy trailer full of strangers,
and if I did get called out on set, I was so far off in the background that
I couldn't even see the movie camera that was supposedly filming me.
The shot would take hours to get right for only a few seconds on the air
– that is if it didn't get edited out completely. Twice I made it on to the
big screen, or should I say the back of my head did. And that's how my
12-year-old self remembered my film and network debut. Not wanting to
repeat history, I told Ryan, "Lots of kids want to be on TV but trust me,
it's not as fun as it looks."

Ryan looked at me strangely and attempted to speak his previous words more clearly, "I don't want to be on TV, I want to take acting classes."

Now put in my place, I discussed it with Mr. Dave and he told me of a great spot called Young Actors Space. It's for kids and young adults who are serious about acting. He said that he attended there as a child and it is still run by the same owner. It was a little pricier than a Lego construction set or a Nerf gun, but it was clearly something Ryan really wanted to try. And it sounded like a better stage for his antics – which currently were being performed nightly at the dinner table.

It turns out Ryan was quite the thespian and after the 10-week-intensive-session, they had a showcase inviting parents and talent agents. Stella from The Savage Agency loved what she saw and requested that Ryan prepare a monologue and come to their office the next weekend. Ryan was thrilled and after spending 10 weeks with kids who were actively going on auditions, he changed his mind about the whole TV thing. The owner of the acting studio said that out of all the kids who didn't yet have representation, Ryan was the only student who got extended an invite from an agency, and Savage was extremely reputable. Understanding that this next step would take things up a notch, I sat Ryan down and we had a serious talk. I reminded him that when he was four he wanted to be a roofer, and when he was five he wanted to work at Legoland, and now he was six and he wanted to be an actor. He heard me out, then offered these words of assurance, "When I grow up I can still work at Legoland. I just want to do acting right now."

I couldn't fight with that logic. The kid clearly had a passion and maybe even a gift.

So I told him he could audition for the agency, but I wanted his monologue to be the Bible verse he recently learned at school, Matthew 28:1-6.

I felt like we should be honest and upfront with this agency as to what kind of family they'd be working with. I also felt that if I invited the Lord to be a part of this from the get-go, He would either clearly open or shut that door. Ryan had no problem with using his already memorized Bible verse as his monologue and he practiced reciting it theatrically every night leading up to his Saturday audition. He went into the interview on his own and when he came back out I asked him how it went. Ryan said, "They told me it would be a blessing if I could be part of their agency."

Honestly, I thought the Bible verse was going to clinch more of a "Thank you but no thank you" kind of response. While it appeared that God was opening this door, I was equal parts excited and scared. His dad and I didn't invest six years of instilling great values into our son just to feed him to the wolves of the entertainment industry. I later told Ryan that I was a little worried because he was still just a kid and a lot of the people who work in Hollywood weren't like the people at church or school. When I went on to mention that many of them don't know Jesus, his quick response was, "Mom, if they don't know about Jesus, I have to tell them." Again with the logic. Okay, I guess we are really doing this.

From ages 6 to 12, Ryan was a true Hollywood actor. We turned down lots of roles that we felt were inappropriate, but I guess when one brings scripture into an agency interview, they know upfront that might happen. Over time, Stella became more like an aunt to Ryan than his talent agent.

She often thanked me for putting his innocence first, as she didn't see that very often in this biz. She pitched him well and he worked a lot, always on wonderful projects. I told Ryan that the best way for others on set to know about Jesus was not by telling them, but showing them. Let's just be ourselves. So we continued to say a

quiet prayer together before meals amidst the sea of cast and crewmembers. And when people would ask me how Ryan got started in acting, I was ready to tell them the truth about Mr. Dave from church, acting classes,

and his Matthew 28 monologue. I recall a few years into all of this, I was chatting with a mom I had just met on set. In the middle of our conversation, she stopped me and said, "Wait, is your kid the one who got an agent by saying a Bible verse?" She went on to tell me she heard about our story from someone on the last project her son worked on. Wow, talk about spreading good news!

Ryan also shined his light in ways only a child could successfully do. He liked wearing his favorite blue t-shirt that read "On fire for Jesus." Most of his days were spent in wardrobe, so he never really had his own clothes on for very long. But he later told me that whenever he wore it, someone would always say, "I like your shirt." Ryan would smile and say, "Thanks, I like it too." He said that's how he would secretly find out who else was "on fire for Jesus" like him. Once a guy from props dropped something and yelled, "Oh, Jesus!" He noticed Ryan standing there and quickly apologized. Ryan said, "It's cool, I don't mind if you bring Jesus on set." The prop guy laughed, but truthfully most people were very conscientious around Ryan. He was friendly and respectful, and they seemed to want to give that to him in return.

But my all-time favorite thing we did on every long-term project he worked on was our "card ministry." I loved taking photos and my son loved meeting new people. So whenever he took a photo with someone on set, we would make two copies of it. We kept one for our album, and one to make that person a card. I told Ryan that I wanted him to really think about what that crewmember's job was, and how he could thank them personally for what they do on set for him. This not only kept Ryan humble and appreciative of others, but the impact these cards made on his cast and crewmates was profound. Many people who work for the studios either don't have much time to spend with their families, or don't have much of a family outside of work. Some of the least likely people were brought to tears by this small gesture that took a moment in time to appreciate them. Some of the crew was shocked when Ryan would ask to take a picture with them. "I should be asking to have my photo taken with you," they would reply. When they got a thank you card the next day with the photo attached, they were speechless. Being so young, Ryan didn't see status. He saw no difference between the lead actress on the show and the guy that wore the cool tape belt marking where people needed to stand. Both had very important jobs and both were very kind to him. Everyone was equal in his eyes. Many people displayed their cards at their workstations or in their dressing rooms, all proudly bearing witness to the fact that they are loved and appreciated.

Acts 1:8

But you will receive power when the Holy Spirit comes on you; and you will be my witnesses in Jerusalem, and in all Judea and Samaria, and to the ends of the earth.

The
Savage
Agency

DIVIDE AND CONQUER

The book of Romans is made up of basic Christian Doctorine **calling for the believing Jews and Gentiles to be unified**, as their desire to glorify Christ is the same. Paul reminds the church that this unity reveals God's righteousness and fulfills His promise to be as one nation under God. Paul's letter concludes with a message to Christians to work out their faith amongst one another, both in the church and in the world.

....

One of my most treasured accomplishments to date was starting In His Arms, a miscarriage and infant loss program for grieving moms. To be truthful, it was the Lord and my 13-week-old baby that actually deserve the credit – but I helped. God used my baby Jeremiah to make such a profound impact, that I gladly took every opportunity to make his miraculous, yet brief, presence in this world known to others, and share the hope I had been given.

I began leading In His Arms at my church in 2013, the year after my miscarriage. Initially, I thought only women would sign up, but God surprised me when five married couples and one grandmother came to the first session. I had already written a six-week curriculum with only hurting moms in mind. As my own husband would rather forget and move on, I didn't stop to think that other husbands may feel different-ly. Sure enough, session after session the group consisted of mostly couples. Even when women would come solo to the group, they really appreciated hearing a man's perspective. It wasn't the dynamic I had planned, but it was even better.

The couples from the very first session were special to me. While they were experiencing the new loss of a baby, I was experiencing the new loss of a marriage. I came alongside them and they came alongside me.

It was so tragic and so inspiring all at once. If you've ever made a close friend during the worst time of your life, you may understand the specialness I'm referring to. Three of these couples stayed on with me as co-leaders and together we continued to lead In His Arms.

One of the couples, Tani and John, had suffered 2 miscarriages and a stillbirth. Sadly, they were never able to have a child together that they could experience here on earth. But in God's ultimate wisdom, it gave them an unmatchable compassion for moms and dads who felt paralyzed from such a loss. Most go through the grieving process and in time move on. But to Tani and John, this ministry was a way that they could celebrate their babies and provide others with the hope that they were fully invested in.

We worked together the next few years to establish a stronger curriculum and market In His Arms to other communities outside of the church. I shared with Tani my desire to write a book together and call it "Dear Baby". We could gather the Dear Baby letters we had asked the moms and dads to write as part of our curriculum, compile them in a book, and publish it for others to read and heal.

In 2016, after my dad suddenly passed and I felt called to care for my mom, leading this class became less of a priority for me. Others had already stepped in to help and we changed the name of the ministry to In Loving Arms, as this encompassed not only God holding us and our babies, but also the members of the group holding each other. With this name change, the timing seemed right for me to step aside and give this support ministry to Tani and John to take over. The two of them made a great team and having a couple lead a couple's group was very beneficial.

Over the next two years I detached myself from the group and moved away with my mom and focused my attention on my new community.

I continued to keep up with In Loving Arms through social media but always felt a little sad that I was not able to continue to be a part of what I had started. At the same time I truly was grateful that hurting parents were able to come find hope and healing through the dedication and perseverance of other leaders.

Then came the spring of 2020. The whole world was strongly encouraged to stay home and isolate due to a pandemic called Covid-19. Caring for my 80-year-old mom with a pre-existing condition, made me discontinue our occasional outside caregiver and just stay home myself. I'd been talking about writing a book for years, perhaps now was my time – no more excuses!

Shortly after my inner self-proclamation, I stumbled upon Tani's social-media post that went something like this:

> *I am excited to share that I have decided to step up and write my first book: <u>Dear Baby</u>*

I kept shaking my head in disbelief as I read on:

> *I have written Dear Baby – Our Angel We Lost, Love and Honor Forever because it is my hope to bring comfort to families impacted by pregnancy and infant loss. You are not alone!*

(Really? Because I feel more alone than ever reading this post!) It went on to say:

> *My book will not be out until October, but you can buy a pre-sale copy by clicking here.*

Looking at the picture of the book with my title and her name on the cover was so surreal. How did it come to this? I handed over my ministry to them, not my book idea. I'm the writer, she's the organized administrator. We had once talked about our two strengths coming together to create something that would help others. I then read the endless comments from her followers, praising her and elevating ~~my~~ her idea.

In my anger, I blasted Tani a hurtful text in which I accused her of stealing my concept and not even bothering to retitle it. She immediately called me. She explained that she had been collecting letters, as we had discussed, since our initial conversation. She felt I had moved away and moved on, and that she wanted to keep her promise to the support group members; that their babies' stories would be told. She offered that if keeping the title we had discussed hurt me she would change it, but said I'd have to decide quickly as it was going to print soon. It took me a few more conversations with her and a couple weeks of fervent prayer before I could come to a place of peace and acceptance. Through God's grace, I began to understand that the truth was - I was never going to actually write Dear Baby. Not that I didn't want to share my story of loss and God's amazing plan for Jeremiah to help others heal, I just wouldn't have reached the ears that needed to hear this as effectively as Tani. I had been 'out of the loop' for some time now. Like me, Tani also had an amazing story to tell and was in a position to collect letters and share about In Loving Arms. I expressed to her that I felt betrayed that she had gotten so far in to the writing process without ever coming to me about it. Tani sincerely apologized for that, and it was then that I was able to let it go. In fact, it was from that place of disappointment and frustration with my own idleness that I forged full speed ahead with this book that you are now reading.

God uses everything for good - if we let Him. There was still a little time before <u>Dear Baby</u> went to print, and Tani wanted me to have a part in it. In addition to my personal "Dear Baby" letter being included in her collection, I also wrote the foreword to her book. As I type this in December 2020, <u>Dear Baby</u> by Tani and John Leeper has been published and distributed to many, including myself. It is a tender story of their journey through loss and concludes with 35 personal letters to babies who were loved, lost, and will always be remembered. I recommend it highly if you or someone you know has experienced such a heartbreak.

I was recently humbled when I received my copy of <u>Dear Baby</u> and noticed this in the acknowledgements:

> *To my friend Kim Preston, I am*
> *eternally grateful for your courage*
> *to start a support group. Thank you*
> *for walking alongside me and John*
> *during the darkest time of our life and*
> *for gently teaching me about a relationship*
> *with God, which led my family back to*
> *church. I am honored to be growing the*
> *seed you planted*

<u>Dear Baby</u> really was a collaborative effort, honoring to the Lord. I understand now that this book was my seed to plant, Tani and John's to water, and God's to grow.

Romans 15:5,6
May the God who gives endurance and encouragement give you a spirit of unity among yourselves as you follow Christ Jesus, so that with one heart and mouth you may glorify the God and Father of our Lord Jesus Christ.

TREASURED

The Apostle Paul writes two letters to the Church of Corinth; first addressing the Corinthians' arrogance and rebellion towards the church, and next **assuring them of his continued commitment and love towards them in spite of their flaws.** He compares our weak, faltered bodies to the unimpressive jars of clay that people in that day would hide their treasures in. By being overlooked on the outside it would not attract attention to what was of true value on the inside. Much like these jars, **the beauty of God within us** is elevated through our own imperfections.

....

Until about the age of 12, I shined in the role of "daddy's little girl." My dad and I had always had a very loving and close relationship. But when my attitude and body began to change, so did my interaction with him. I wasn't a little girl anymore and I'm sure my dad felt he was keeping the peace and honoring me as he backed away a bit. But deep down I no longer felt treasured. I didn't know it then, but became keenly aware of it much later as I looked back on my youth. As a pre-teen, I gauged much of my self-worth on my outward appearance and began to place little value on the beauty that lay within me. By the age of 14, I had a boyfriend and began to seek out an identity for myself in this new relationship. We liked how our two *clay* jars looked and felt along side each other, never truly caring how different we actually were on the inside. When it came to falling in love, we had no idea what we were looking for and we seemed to just figure it out as we went.

Years later, after I was married, a friend and I were talking about dating life prior to marriage. She told me that as a child and up into her teens, her dad would take her on daddy-daughter dates. She felt that it had been really helpful before actually dating. I wished I had that experience as a young girl growing up. I think it may have made a difference to spend some time as a teenager being valued by a man who truly knows and loves me for the treasure that I am. I don't blame my dad for allowing me to break away from him. He did the very best he could with the knowledge that he had. I just wish I could go back in time and help him understand me – now that I finally do. If I could, this is what I'd tell him:

Dear Daddy,
(A note from your pre-teen daughter)
Oh how I loved being your little girl. You carried me when my little legs grew tired, you wiped my tears away when I was hurt or upset, you spoiled me when Mommy wasn't looking. You told me how pretty I was each time I got dressed up. You protected me in your strong arms during the scary parts of the movie. You hugged me and kissed me without needing a reason at all.

I never questioned your love for me. I always felt beautiful in your eyes, even when I didn't brush my hair or was sick in bed with the flu. I never feared falling, for I knew you would catch me every time. You were the most important man in my life and I secretly felt sorry for Mom, for I knew when I grew up that I was going to marry you (but Mom's a giver and she'll be okay).

The thing is…as I now approach my teenage years, I feel this internal conflict I can't make sense of, let alone articulate to you.

The "yucky boys" are becoming rather cute and my clothes don't fit the same on me anymore. I no longer tell you my secrets because you might think less of me. When I'm not giving you the silent treatment or rolling my eyes, I will say things to you like, "You don't get it!" "You're embarrassing me!" or " I'm not a little girl!"

The truth is I don't truly mean any of those things. Perhaps I say them because I am confused or mad that you can't fix my problems anymore. After all, you've always been able to fix everything from a broken toy to a broken heart. Maybe I say those things because I want to test you, I feel myself changing and I wonder will people still love me if I'm not the same? Subconsciously I put up a wall, I make it hard to love me in order to find out if your love has limits and at what point am I too much to take?

It's different with Mom. She knows what it feels like to grow little bumps on her chest, to be grossed out by this new monthly occurrence known as "our cycle," and what it's like to start crying over something completely insignificant. But you, Daddy, you don't know me that way. I'm suddenly not the same little girl you would twirl in the living room or carry to bed when I fell asleep on your lap. But deep down, there are days I want to go back to being her. I won't actually tell you that, I'll assume you already know, for as my dad you know everything.

When I look in the mirror at my maturing, awkward body, and the pimples that cover my once-peaches and cream skin, I wonder who would ever want to kiss this cheek. What guy would ever find me pretty? I know that I look and act differently, but I find comfort in knowing that I'll always be your little girl despite my outward appearance.

It must be hard for you too, wanting to love me like you always have, yet respect me as a blossoming young woman. My sporadic emotional outbursts, or sudden withdrawing probably makes you wonder if I'm possessed. Maybe you feel you should stop kissing, hugging, and holding me, thinking that that's what I want or maybe you pull away to not remind yourself that I am growing up. But here's the thing. I need to feel loved by you now more than ever. My body is not only changing on the outside but I'm somehow going through open-heart surgery and a lobotomy all at the same time! I crave positive, male attention, as it counteracts the self-inflicted lie that I'm the ugliest, weirdest, most insecure girl in all of middle school. Basically, if you don't kiss my pimpled cheek, I will hope that someone else will. If you don't endure my meltdown over what I deem tragic, I will instinctively seek out a guy who is willing to listen. If you don't take me out on a date to show me how a lady should be treated, someone else will set that standard for me. I know I'm not very loveable right now, but Daddy, don't give up on me! I need to learn that a man who truly loves me doesn't shut me out when things get tough. Please fight for me.

Love,
Your little girl, in a teenage body

This letter was actually taken from one of my journals from years ago. More recently, each time I sit down to read my Bible, I feel like I'm finally getting that daddy-daughter date I've always longed for. It's like the Lord dusts off my clay jar and pours out the treasures inside. We spend some time together shining up a gem or two and He reminds me of the beautiful gifts He has given me that can only be seen when I open up the lid of my heart and share with others the powerful treasures that lie within. I'm not sure if I'll ever marry again, but if I do, it will be to a Christ-like man who looks beyond the jar and values what's inside.

2 Corinthians 4:7
But we have this treasure in jars of clay to show that this
all-surpassing power is from God and not from us.

PETALS FROM HEAVEN

The Book of Galatians is another letter written by the Apostle Paul, this time to the churches in Galatia. Paul speaks with the Lord's authority explaining that it's not the law of the Torah that justifies our beliefs as Christians, but the gospel of Jesus. Through Jesus we are added to a new family and equipped by the Holy Spirit to love God and love others. **The only thing that counts is faith expressing itself through love. (Galatians 5:6)**

....

I never really intended anyone to read my "Dear Baby" letter that I shared with you in "Psalms." I wrote it with only my baby in mind the morning after I miscarried. It took me over three hours and an entire tissue box to get through it. But when I was done, I felt a peace that could only come from opening my heart up and letting some of that pain go. The letter was meant just for me, as a way to honor my baby and begin to say goodbye.

Before that weekend was over, I began to realize that I'd somehow eventually have to tell others about God's change in plans. I felt a tug on my heart to send my letter and photo to the ladies in my weekly women's Bible study. I knew they'd view my baby's photo through the eyes of his Creator so they seemed like a safe start. Back then I was much more private and sharing something that personal was way out of my comfort zone. So I was relieved by their outpouring of love in response to my group email. I knew they wouldn't see my letter and photo as inappropriate, but I didn't expect them to be equally as amazed and inspired as I was by this little life.

After feeling blessed by the comforting words of my wonderful sisters-in-Christ, I decided to send the letter and photo on to the members of my immediate family and closest girlfriends from over the years. This felt a little more vulnerable because many of the people in this next group did not share in my Christian beliefs. Would my 13-week-old baby be seen as nothing more than an unfinished science experiment? Nevertheless, I knew they all loved me and I wanted them to know what happened beyond "Kim lost her baby." They too were greatly impacted and told me they couldn't get over how precious he was when they reached out to comfort me.

At first, I questioned God's timing and wished I had never put my pregnancy announcement on social media at the 12-week mark. It felt like God had waited for me to attach myself to this little life, share this joy with everyone, only to have me go back and humbly say, "Nevermind." Seven days after my joyful announcement post, I now wrote a new post that simply read, "Sadly, our family learned this weekend how fragile life is."

Thankfully, the post didn't warrant a single "like." Instead, comments and messages of prayer, love, and support began pouring in on a continual basis. My heart felt as if it would burst. I had no idea so many people had that much compassion for me and were so pained by my suffering. People who I had never even heard acknowledge God, publicly stated that I would be included in their prayers.

Galatians 6:2 tells us to bear each others burdens, and that was exactly what happened. Each person who invested themself in my story was hurting too. Somehow, knowing others were carrying my pain along with me, made it not as heavy. I had mentioned in my general post that I had taken an unbelievable photo and written a letter to remember him by. Many asked if I would privately share my letter and baby's photo with them. From there, some went on to express the desire to share it with someone they knew who would be blessed by reading it too. Cards, letters, and emails thanking me for sharing something so personal began flooding my inbox and my actual mailbox. Many shared personal details of their own past losses. Some were close friends, but there were others I had never experienced a bond with until now. Women of various ages, from different circles of my life, identified with the loss of a child. Whether their baby died through a miscarriage or an abortion, the proof of life through my baby's photo was indisputable. I was surprised by comments like, "If I had seen that photo of your baby when I was a teen, my child would be 30 years old today." Another friend called me weeping. She told me that for 15 years she had been pushing away the pain of her own miscarriage. After reading the letter and seeing exactly what her 13-week old fetus must have also looked like, she would now proudly share she has three children, not just her two here on Earth.

A few days after I had posted about my miscarriage, a delivery service brought me a dozen tulips. The card simply read:

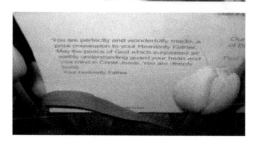

You are perfectly and wonderfully made, a prized possession to your Heavenly Father. May the peace of God that surpasses all earthly understanding guard your heart and your mind in Christ Jesus. You are deeply loved. Your Heavenly Father

To this very day, I have no idea which *earthly angel* God used to send me those flowers, and I'm actually glad about that. I believe He placed the idea in someone's heart, and for me knowing the "middleman" is less important. Those flowers are from God, delivered straight to my doorstep!

After reading "Dear Baby," a friend told me, "I can't believe your strength and willingness to write and share such a personal story – I would have just crawled in a hole and shut down for a few weeks." Honestly, I would have thought that would have been my reaction too. But when I woke up the morning after I miscarried, staying under the covers was not an option. I could feel the weight of the Holy Spirit on my heart, telling me, "Go write!" It was as if I would never breathe properly again until I did. And since that day, I've never stopped writing.

Galatians 6:2,10

Carry each other's burdens, and in this way you will fulfill the law of Christ. Therefore, as we have opportunity, let us do good to all people, especially to those who belong to the family of believers.

IMMEASURABLY MORE

Paul writes the Book of Ephesians from prison to the people of Ephesus. Paul shares that God's plan has always been for His people to be unified as one in a multi-cultural family. Paul invites his readers to experience **God's grace, love, and mercy through the power of the gospel.** He desires everyone to discover the joy of all that God has for them.

....

Ephesians 3:20
Now to Him who is able to do immeasurably more than we ask or imagine, according to His power that is at work within us, to Him be the glory.

This verse was given to us by our mission trip's spiritual leader, Sandi, the day we landed in Uganda. She asked us to really meditate on it throughout our time there and see if we could apply it to our own experiences. I woke up early the following morning on Monday July 30, 2007. I was way too excited to sleep. Today was the day a few of us would travel to the town of Deo to meet our sponsored children. Our family had been writing and praying for nine-year-old Ronald for almost a year now. I was anxious to know if this whole idea of "give $30 a month and give a child hope for the future" was all that it was promised to be. I was well-prepared with a backpack full of school supplies and letters from my two sons to present to Ronald upon my arrival. In addition, I also had gifts and letters for four other African children. My friends Tricia, Amanda, Shelley and Annette had all given me items for their sponsored children who attended this school in Deo as well.

Due to my excitement, I found myself sitting on the bathroom floor in our motel at 5 a.m. journaling my thoughts. I didn't want to wake my roommate so it was that, or try to lie still in a bed under a mosquito net for another hour. I had stuffed the paper with the verse on it in my journal the night before. When I came across it, I thought about how it would apply to my upcoming experience. If God would allow me to be able to see all five of these children, take pictures with each of them, and then honestly report back to others that we really were making a difference in these lives - what more could I ask for? Yet, the verse says, *more than we ask or imagine*. Hmm, so according to God, not only will my prayer be answered, but additional blessings that I can't even imagine will also be occurring. I consider myself a faithful servant (I mean after all, I'm praying on the bathroom floor at 5 a.m. in AFRICA!) But still, if God could just pull off my initial request, I would be amazed.

The moment had finally arrived and I joined four other hopeful sponsors from our mission team in a Jeep traveling to Deo. Between the five of us, we were prepared to see 12 children who had no idea that we were coming. After an hour drive in the rain, we pulled into the school parking lot/ play yard that was nothing but dirt. The students were all in blue uniforms playing happily on a large flat area, boys in pants and collared shirts and

girls in modest dresses. The only thing on the yard (besides well-dressed children and dirt) was a single ball. Yet everyone seemed happy and amused. As I opened the door of the Jeep, the thickness of the humid air hit me like a warm  washcloth. But then, there to greet me was a small boy in a red-striped shirt with a refreshing smile. I remember thinking, "He's awfully happy for a boy who neglected to put on his uniform this morning." I knew I'd run into children that I wouldn't have a gift for. So, thankfully I had a large roll of stickers with me, and apparently this was my first customer.

I handed him a sticker. His smile got even bigger and he proudly stuck it to the middle of his forehead.

The administrator of the school was a stunning, poised African woman with a radiant smile. She greeted us warmly despite not knowing we were coming. We handed her our list of hopefuls. Before she got to work on collecting the children, she led us to an empty classroom with four cement walls, a thatched roof, and more dirt. To my surprise, the news of the "sticker lady" was already out! A group of children soon circled me as I walked. They were all pointing to their foreheads. As I held tightly onto the five sets of pre-assigned gifts, I managed to peel off stickers and say the words "God bless you" as I attached one to each child's forehead. Most of the children either said, "God bless you too" or "thank you" before running back to their classes. Soon all had dispersed leaving only "the red shirt boy" at my side. He smiled, put his finger up and said, "one more." How could I refuse? I stuck another to his forehead and caught up with my colleagues. As I was approaching the room the administrator had prepared for us to wait in, I noticed that my new friend was still with me. I bent down and held out yet another sticker. This time, I put it on his finger and said, "This one's to share. Go find a friend who doesn't have one."

Proud of my quick, creative thinking, I turned and entered the room where we would wait in anticipation for our sponsored children to be brought to us. There were four wooden benches positioned into a square for my teammates and I to sit. I grabbed a seat on the bench and looked up to find "the red shirt boy" standing directly in front of me, only now with three stickers on his forehead (sigh). He then took the spot next to me. I knew he probably wasn't supposed to be in here, but today I was not in charge, so I decided to just enjoy having a sidekick 'til he got caught.

Children began to arrive one by one. The administrator sweetly introduced them to us and once the child looked comfortable, she'd leave to go and get another. All of the kids were so well-mannered and naturally, pretty shy. I met Tricia and Shelley's girls first, and even though I was not their real sponsored parent, they were just as happy to see me. They loved getting gifts and letters and posed for pictures that I could take back to their American family. This whole time "the red shirt boy" was sitting to my right watching all that was going on and nobody seemed to know he existed but me. My sponsored child, Ronald, entered the room looking very nervous and silent. At first I thought he didn't speak English. (Ugandan is the primary language, but once they are in school, English is taught and used.) Together, we went through the contents of the backpack I had brought him. I pulled out Blake and Ryan's letters to him and began reading. By the second sentence, he joined me in reading out loud and actually read quite well. I asked if he had just started school this year when I became his spon-sor. He quietly communicated to me that he had had a sponsor before, but for some reason they stopped sponsoring him. Ronald's accent was thick but with some highly concentrated, careful listening, I was able to decipher that because he was doing so well in school, the ARM program allowed him to stay, in hopes that another family would come forward and provide support. I now understood that we were that family. I had thought it odd that he already had a uniform shirt on in his sponsorship card photo. I remember that day at church, when I told Ryan that he could pick one child from the stack of sponsorship cards to be his ad-opted brother or sister from Africa. Ryan later told me, "I chose Ronald because he was dressed nicer than the children in all the other photos."

In my naiveté, I secretly wondered if the program was double-dipping on these African kids in order to bring in more money. But now it all made sense. Having already been left by one sponsor, I could only imagine how he must have felt meeting his second sponsor. He

was probably thinking that I wouldn't like him or that he might say the wrong things. Poor kid. We talked about his family (five brothers and one sister) and then we took some pictures together.

I even let "the red shirt boy" use a camera for the first time and take a photo of Ronald and I. Suddenly it hit me! He was wearing a red shirt because he doesn't even go to this school. That's why no one is looking for him. I knelt down and looked him in the eyes. "Do you have a sponsor?" I asked. He could no longer look at me as he shook his head "no." He probably thought he would be sent home and forced to stop living vicariously through the students enrolled here. Without hesitation I asked, "Would you like me to sponsor you?"

He took my hand and humbly whispered, "Thank you." I had brought a small teddy bear as extra to give to one of the five sponsored children I had come to visit. But I realized then that the bear was intended for him. He had been eyeing it throughout my visit, but never touched it or asked about it. I gently pushed the bear into his chest and said, "This is for you." Again, a whispered "thank you."

When the administrator returned, I inquired about "the red shirt boy." She said she was so busy finding the sponsored children that she hadn't realized he was with us in the room this whole time. She went on to tell me that he lives in the area and is being raised by his grandfather. Because of his situation and sweet spirit, she has developed a soft spot for him. He doesn't attend the school, but often visits to be around other kids. She said that his grandfather would be so happy and that I would really bless this family by sponsoring him. I informed her that I was the one who was blessed, for I did not choose him, but he chose me.

Cheryl, a volunteer from the ARM Organization we were traveling with, was a little concerned that I had already told the boy I would sponsor him. She said sometimes people feel that way when they are here in Uganda, but then go home and change their minds. Children are left devastated and feel rejected. I assured her this would not be the case with me. The administrator wrote down the info I needed and told me: He is six years old, and his name is Arafat. Wow! I had heard that 85% of Ugandans consider themselves Christian, 10% Muslim and the other 5% practice other beliefs such as witchcraft. Well, apparently his legal guardian would feel blessed if he went to this Christian school, so if he is Muslim, he's about to meet Jesus in a whole new way.

The rain was now coming down in buckets and the team was trying to all pile back into the Jeep. The administrator was going to accompany us up to the preschool where the remaining four of the 12 children were waiting for us. As I looked up from my spot in the back of the Jeep, I saw Arafat clutching his bear and crying loudly. The administrator said, "He is crying because you are leaving." My heart sank. All I could think to do was pass up a sticker to Cheryl who was sitting by the window. She rolled it down and as the rain beat in, stretched out her arm to Arafat and said, "This is from Mama Kim." He quickly took the sticker and added it to his well-displayed collection on his forehead, although the crying did not stop. Our driver (who I later learned was Cheryl's sponsored child for the last seven years and was now going to university) gave Arafat a Ugandan coin in exchange for a smile. We drove away and I couldn't help but praise God for giving me immeasurably more than I asked or imagined.

Ephesians 3:16-19

I pray that out of glorious riches He may strengthen you with power through His Spirit in your inner being, so that Christ may dwell in your hearts through faith. And I pray that you, being rooted and established in love, may have power together with all the Lord's holy people, to grasp how wide and long and high and deep is the love of Christ, and to know this love that surpasses knowledge- that you may be filled to the measure of all the fullness of God.

Update

In 2015 I would travel to Uganda again and was blessed to visit Ronald and Arafat in their homes. Ronald's family took the only wall decorations they had and insisted I take them home as a gift. Arafat never stopped smiling and repeatedly asked me one question, "When are you coming back?"

While they have since finished school and I no longer serve as their sponsor, I am better for knowing them and pray my presence in their lives made an impact too.

ALOHA

Paul was originally imprisoned for publicly sharing about Jesus. While prison is not what he would have wished for, he sees that his ministry is far from over and his new situation can still be for the good of the Lord. He continues writing letters and speaking openly about the love of Jesus from his cell to other prisoners and guards. Paul shares a profound perspective in his letter to the Philippians, that **to live is Christ but to die is gain**. This is to remind us as Christians that death means the reward of Heaven, but until then we **live a life that glorifies Him.**

....

July 19, 2012 was six months after my miscarriage, and what would have been my due date. Being the awesome God that He is, full of hope, love, and grace, why would I be surprised that He had something very special planned for me that week? Let me first back up a few months to December 2011. My husband had some exciting news for our family. He worked with a company that decided to hold a raffle for executive recruiters who made successful placements within their firm that year. Three names would be chosen out of a hat and each of these recruiters would receive a $2,500 vacation voucher to use however they wished. Well through the grace of God, nine of my husband's candidates were placed within this company in 2011. This meant his name would be entered nine times into the raffle. Needless to say, his odds were pretty good. In fact, so good, that his name was chosen two out of the three times. If you've already done the math, you know that means $5,000 in vacation money! As excited as we all were, there was a reality that needed to be faced: I was eight weeks pregnant and the voucher had to be used within one year. With our boys in the throws of middle school and a baby arriving mid-summer, this was going to be tricky. We called the company, told them our situation and hoped we might get an extension on the time restriction. Instead, they said that we could cash in the voucher and just take the money. Yippee! Having not foreseen this pregnancy, our insurance plan covered few prenatal expenses. So we put this money aside and gave it the name "Hospital Bill." Now, fast-forward to the last week of May 2012. We suddenly realized that while there would not be a baby this summer, there could still be a vacation. But June was already around the corner, and a vacation for four would take some research and planning. I had so much going on with Blake's eighth grade graduation and the chaos that comes with end-of-the-year activities, I just didn't have time to organize a family trip. It was at this point that God decided to make His big reveal. Scrolling through Facebook, I noticed a status my friend Kelli had just posted three minutes prior:

> *Hello FB Friends...*
> *I am looking to sell our timeshare week in Maui... The week of July 20th-27th, on Ka'anapali Shore...BEAUTIFUL!!!*

I quickly made sure I was the first to reply: Interested! I then ran to my calendar to check if the dates would work. When I realized how perfect the timing truly would be, my heart was filled with the knowledge that I am loved and He has not forgotten. You see, I had been handling the loss of our baby pretty well. But for some reason I had been dreading the week our baby would have been born. I found myself praying, "Please Lord, I don't want to become consumed with bitterness while cleaning my bathrooms or running errands across the 105-degree Valley, wishing I was experiencing the joy of a new baby." Oh how special it would now be to experience something amazing with what I have, instead of being focused on what I have not.

As all the vacation details were coming together, I couldn't help but see God's hand over the details. We used some of the money from our friend "Hospital Bill" to send Kelli the $1,800 for our spacious two-bedroom villa for seven nights. After pricing airline tickets online, the best deal we could get was $800 a person, round trip (let me help you with the math this time), totaling exactly $5,000. This vacation was our gift from God, in celebration of not only the small, impactful life of our baby in Heaven - but to appreciate the lives of our family here together!

Early on in this journey, in the depths of my heartache, I remember praising God, "For out of all my children, if You had to take one to Heaven early, thank you for allowing it to be the one I hadn't met yet." (Never underestimate the power of perspective.) On this trip, I truly enjoyed what I had to the greatest of my ability. Having another child would have been a blessing, but it would have also meant missing out on some family adventures in order to "stay back" and care for a little one. My boys were 12 and 14, such great ages to get out and explore. So I biked down a volcano at sunrise, snorkeled on a good hair day, and took in every valuable minute I had with my gifts from above.

According to Wikipedia, "aloha" is the Hawaiian word encompassing love, affection, peace, compassion, and mercy. It is commonly used as a simple greeting, but has a deeper cultural and spiritual significance to Native Hawaiians, for whom the term is used to define a force that holds together existence. The Lord showed us "Aloha" throughout this trip, in fact everywhere we went there were signs welcoming us to paradise. It made me recall that our baby was experiencing paradise too, and one far greater than anything we could imagine.

Philippians 1:9,10

And this is my prayer: that your love may abound more and more in knowledge and depth of insight, so that you will be able to discern what is best and may be pure and blameless until the day of Christ.

WHO'S YOUR DADDY

Paul continues to reach out to his brothers and sisters in Christ from imprisonment. Here he encourages the church of Colossae to keep strong in the faith, despite cultural pressures to turn away from who Jesus truly is. They are to **stay committed to holy living, so as not to be deceived by fine-sounding arguments**. Paul gives clear characteristics of a Christian family: wives who **submit,** husbands who **love,** and children who **obey.** These things should be done in respect to the Lord, for He is the piece that will bring peace to your home.

While the word "submit" is not highlighted in the paragraph above, I'm going to guess it is the word that stood out to you the most. It's a tough one for many, and it was for me in my marriage. In revisiting this instruction in Colossians 3, I saw something I hadn't understood before. Here Paul is addressing Christian households. Therefore, the husband of that household is in submission to the Lord's guidance and teachings. Otherwise, a Christian wife would be submitting to a husband who is acting independently of the Lord, and this is not how God intended it. **Ecclesiastes 4:12** reminds us that **a cord of three strands is not quickly broken.**

Not too long ago, I recall one of my sons telling me about a girl he met at school. He said, "Mom, you would really like her for me, she's a strong Christian." His statement gave me pause. A few years back, this may have really excited me but having had my own marriage end largely because of our differing religious views, it altered my reaction. I explained to my son that what I would really like for him is to find interest in a girl whose faith matched his own, hence being equally yoked. It would be unfair for me to desire someone for him who would carry the burden of increasing his faith. My greatest happiness would be for him to start out in complete spiritual agreement with his future mate and from there they could grow together.

Many of my stories in this book are of my two young boys and their unwavering faith in Jesus. Perhaps those stories came to mind because they are my favorite ones to think back on and I appreciate them more now that things are a bit different. I miss the days of their youth when my words were golden to them.

I sense that having been their teacher as well as their mom, gave me an extra dose of credibility in their eyes. I taught my boys to be independent thinkers and unafraid to stand up for what they believe. So I suppose I should be proud of them for questioning the beliefs they were raised with and wanting to find their own personal conviction that they can stand on. These days there is less evidence of that child-like faith they once exhibited, and more openness to alternative ideas on faith and who God is. It's not something they wish to discuss, so I've decided to pray instead of press. But in true mom form, I wonder if I went wrong somewhere: Perhaps my strong stance combined with their dad's uncertainty made their clear Christian faith cloudy. Or maybe the divorce came at a time that made them question everything they once believed in and were told to be true. Or perhaps inevitably as young adults, they have been presented with conflicting views that have made them want to step away and truly figure faith out for themselves. But the reason itself doesn't actually matter. They are both at an age where they are accountable for the personal path they choose to walk down. They know I pray for them and am available if they want to talk with me, but as their mom I choose to be at peace. I don't know where their walk is with the Lord, but I trust that He is still walking with them. I have this photo that hangs above my desk that takes me back to a

treasured place in time when my boys were 8 and 10. It was a time that our family unit felt strong and in their own desire, they both asked to be baptized. Their dad, along with our pastor, baptized them at church and I got a front row seat to a moment I will never forget. It wasn't the act of them going under water that gave me such joy, but their certain proclamation of faith just before they were submerged.

Both of my boys have always told me that they clearly see how much my faith in God has helped me through hard times over the years. From time to time (usually on long car trips when no one can walk away), we respectfully debate theology. I try to understand their intellect and they try to respect my heart. I remember Ryan once stopping mid-sentence and saying, "I know how important your faith is to you, and I hesitate to say something that will put that into question." I smiled to know how much my son cared, but then giggled at the thought of someone having the ability to make me question my faith. I explained to him that when I was his age perhaps that might have been a possibility, but given the vast amount of experiences that God has brought me through, my faith is now unshakable. I don't need rationale or sound logic to explain my beliefs, I've seen firsthand what God my Father, Jesus my Brother, and the Holy Spirit my Helpmate, have done in my life. That is why my faith can never be hindered by another. I may not be able to make you understand what I believe, but there is nothing you can do or say that can take that belief away from me. Time and experience were powerful tools for me, as I'm sure they will be for my sons. The more opportunities God has to show up in their circumstances and shine a light that can only come from His divine intervention, the more they'll understand that He is the same loving God of their youth. People may change, but God never will.

Colossians 2:2,3
My goal is that they may be encouraged in heart and united in love, so that they may have the full riches of complete understanding, in order that they may know the mystery of God, namely, Christ, in whom are hidden all the treasures of wisdom and knowledge.

THE GRATITUDE GAME

In Paul's letter to the people of Thessalonica, he praises them for **welcoming the Gospel's message with joy in spite of their sufferings.** In this, we see that following Jesus exhibits a way of life that is counter-cultural to this world. The Thessalonians were an excellent example of **responding to hostility and adversity with love and generosity.**

....

Have you ever had one of those days where nothing goes right? A day you can't wait to be over, where if one more thing goes wrong, there is an excellent chance you will have a complete meltdown? I recently had one of those days and as I sit back and recall each grueling detail, a smile comes to my face and I am grateful for every moment of that experience.

It was 2 p.m. on a hot Friday afternoon. My two boys and I had been visiting my sister and their little cousins in Orange County. As we packed up to leave, my husband called to tell me that Ryan had an audition for a TV show at 3:30 p.m. that day. I grumbled a bit as he went on to explain that the audition location was on our way home and the casting agency needed to fill the role immediately. I know I should have been happy that Ryan got opportunities to exercise his craft, but the thought of driving, parking, and waiting around just didn't sound appealing after an already long day. Despite my poor attitude, I loaded the boys and our loot into the car to head out to Hollywood.

I don't know about you, but when my attitude is poor, even the little things become burdensome hurdles that upset me even more. Finding myself wanting to yell at my children and be grouchy and negative, I came up with a game. It has since been dubbed "the gratitude game." I explained to my boys that every time something didn't go our way, we needed to thank God for it in the most appreciative way we could muster up. After all, God tells us "to give thanks in all circumstances." Yes, I recalled this verse and happily quoted it to my children, but on the inside I was more like a child myself - saying to her Father above, "I don't get your rule, it makes no sense to me, but because you're my Dad I'm gonna do it." My intention wasn't to mock God, but as I look back on this journey, it was clear that I had very little faith that being thankful would make any difference. Nevertheless, I took my mustard-seed-sized faith and buckled up.

We hadn't even backed out of my sister's driveway when I was given the joy of officially starting the game.

> "Thank you Lord that our gas tank is empty and I must now stop and use a portion of our valuable time to fuel up," I began.

The boys giggled and the game continued.

> "Thank you God that my brother is playing on the DS game and I get to read while I wait for my turn," Blake chimed in.

Then Ryan. "Thank you that the battery just died in the DS and now neither of us gets to play."

The game proved to be challenging, but the boys caught on quickly. Once our gas tank was full and we hopped on the freeway, the game hit high gear even though our speed didn't. *Thank you Lord for the air conditioning in our comfortable car as we sit through this bumper-to-bumper traffic. Thank you that we saw a license plate from Maine. Thank you that the driver next to us picking his nose didn't eat it* (sorry – just a Boy Mom keepin' it real). The next hour was filled with laughter and silliness that I'm sure is a rarity on the 5 Freeway on a hot Friday afternoon. Before we knew it, it was 3:30 p.m. (Ryan's call time) and we were just approaching our exit off the freeway. A very large, slow truck was in front of us and we ended up following the brown smoke from its exhaust through a two-mile series of right-hand turns that eventually led to our designated street.

At one point, we entertained the thought that this truck driver must also be trying out for the part of "Boy #1." The mere mention of this made us laugh so hard that the three of us were reminded that we all were about to pee our pants. Oops, almost forgot *thank you Lord that we didn't!* And while I'm at it, *thank you that the street that the audition is on is completely closed off due to construction.* "How exciting!" I said. "It's like a maze. We just need to work our way through traffic to find the other side of our street located who knows where to get to our desired destination." It was like a video game challenge. Instead of tackling it through the glare of a 3x2-inch screen on their DS, we were living it - 4D! *Thanks again!*

When we finally got there, we all cheered. *Praise God! ...and thank you for the closest parking spot being just three blocks away.* Although it is difficult to walk when you "really gotta go," we appreciated the exercise after nearly two hours of sitting. Believe it or not, we were still finding joy in this game. We walked through the casting office doors at 4:10 p.m. I could tell by the emptiness of the room that the auditions were over -we missed it. I tried to hide my disappointment as I wrote Ryan's name on the call-sheet. I noticed the last kid that signed in was there at 4:00. We were so close. I didn't have the heart to tell the boys our trip was all for nothing. For a few moments I took a personal break from the gratitude game and began playing the "if only game." If only we had a closer parking spot. If only the street wasn't closed off. If only that truck had been behind me and not in front of me. If only I had put gas in the car yesterday. If only... I soon realized this game was not nearly as enjoyable. Not wanting to ask the boys to join me in my pity party, I quickly decided to rejoin them in the gratitude game.

The truth is there may have been some sarcastic "thank yous"along the way, but the laughter and bonding I shared with my sons was genuine. All those "if onlys" added up to a fun and memorable afternoon. Somewhere along the 5 Freeway my mustard seed began to sprout. Despite my disappointment, I now had all the faith in the world that God was going to get us out of this with smiles on our faces.

> We took turns using the restroom (*Thank you God!*) and played a game of "I Spy." Eventually, a woman appeared in the doorway, somewhat surprised to see us. While I was certain the role had already been given out, she sweetly called Ryan into an adjacent room and went through the audition motions anyway. When Ryan came back out he was smiling. (I was thankful for that). The three of us walked towards the exit and noticed a basket full of colorful lollipops that were clearly there for the taking. We each reached in and grabbed one. As we walked out the door, Ryan had one final praise, *Thank you God that we came all this way for a sucker.* I can't remember ever being with my boys and laughing together so hard. Our bellies rolled all the way to the car, at which point we agreed this was the best game ever!

I later asked Ryan what happened behind that audition door. Ironically, all Boy #1 had to say was the word "no." Wanting a natural response, the casting agent asked Ryan, "Can you name all 50 states and their capitals?" Ryan thought for a moment and said, "I can try." Of course he said that. After hours of trying to be positive, he couldn't help but make the best of his situation.

> *Thank you Lord for this valuable lesson. Thank you that the journey to learn the lesson had you next to us, entertaining us each step of the way. Thank you for making it fun and for giving me such a fond memory with my boys.*

I Thessalonians 5:16-18
Be joyful always; pray continually; give thanks in all circumstances,
for this is God's will for you in Christ Jesus

THE TIMOTHY AWARD

First and Second Timothy are actually two letters written by Paul, and addressed to young Timothy. Paul knew Timothy's heart for the Lord, so he calls him to boldly go to Ephesus and teach the people there to turn from their corrupt ways. No one tells Paul that Timothy is worthy of this task. **Paul recognizes Timothy's sincere faith** and knows with confidence what he is capable of.

As an elementary school teacher, I have often experienced parents informing me that their child is "very special" in some way, but I wish they hadn't. I'm referring to the "specialness" that a parent feels their child possesses that goes beyond other children's "specialness." When I was a young teacher with no children of my own yet, I hadn't really understood this parental right of passage. I mean molding and nurturing someone from a formless being to a high functioning little human is no small feat. But when I'm about to spend six hours a day, five days a week with your child, I'd like to get to know them without any precon- ceived notions. I wish back then that I was bold enough to give par- ents this piece of advice: Don't rob yourself of the joy of letting others discover the "specialness" in your child. If you tell people your child is special in some way, that gift now becomes an expectation rather than a pleasant surprise. And once your prodigy is placed in the same classroom as all the other prodigies, things usually look a little different.

Years later, I too became a mom and it was then that I completely understood the strong desire to give an introduction for one's child. (But seriously...mine truly was special!) From the time our first son, Blake, was a year old until I literally followed him to Kindergarten as his teacher, my husband and I operated a tutoring business. Books, flashcards, and educational games were a big part of my son's early environment. As a result, he learned to read very quickly and by the time he started preschool at age three, he could sight-read many words. He was what they call a "natural reader." Okay, enough of me being "that parent." Here comes the humbling part... About two weeks into starting school, the preschool director mentions how obedient and sweet Blake is. While this was a nice compliment to hear, I was a little deflated by its generalness. I mean, lots of three-year-olds are sweet and some even obedient... but mine can READ!

> Yes, I ignored my own advice and voluntarily blurted out, "Have you heard him read yet?"

> "Read?" she asked. "I actually haven't heard him say more than a handful of words since school started. He's very shy in class and when he does speak, it's so soft that I can barely hear him."

As a young mom, I was dumbfounded. Here I was thinking my son could very well start college after elementary school, and the truth was he was struggling to perform at age-appropriate tasks. I had been so enamored with his reading ability that I neglected to foster a skill so basic and foundational. So that year I became motivated to let Blake's words speak to who he is. I never realized how much I enabled his shyness by speaking up for him. It's so much easier to recognize such parenting flaws in others than it is to see it in yourself. I needed to hold on to that truth.

A little over-whelmed

That first year of Monday/Wednesday/Friday half-day preschool was a growing time for both of us. Blake even got an award for being an "independent walker to class" because he was one of the few preschoolers that could follow the teacher all the way from the play yard to the classroom without a parent chaperone. But let's face it. This was actually an award for me. It took every ounce of strength to not be one of those parents who walks their child all the way to the door everyday. Not that I judge those who do, but I knew I had to start doing little things to foster independence in my shy boy. I told Blake early on that I was going to say goodbye from the yard because it made me sad to hear kids cry when their parents left them at the classroom door. That somehow made perfect sense to him. On occasion when his dad took him to school, he did get walked all the way ("cause Daddy doesn't care if other kids cry").

Two years later when Blake graduated from preschool, the children put on a program for all the parents along with an award ceremony. There was the "Best Helper Award," "The Best Artist Award," "The Love for Jesus Award" and so-on.

I was excited and curious to hear which category Blake's teachers chose to elevate him. Finally, Blake was called up to the stage and presented "The Timothy Award." I'm not going to lie, I didn't understand. What the heck kind of award is that? All I could remember about Timothy in the Bible is that he was timid and my boy is so much more than that. I casually bumped into (but wanted to body slam) the preschool director afterwards at the juice-and-cookie reception. She mentioned how perfectly deserving Blake was of the Timothy Award. It was then that I asked her if she could please explain it to me. She said that Timothy was believed to be the soft-spoken disciple of Paul, but he was actually quite the leader and whenever he spoke, his words were full of wisdom.

I couldn't have been more proud. Two years prior, I had taken it upon myself to inform this very same teacher that my son was on the smarter side. Today, she one-upped me, awarding him for being bold in his wisdom. I'm so glad I didn't rob myself of that joy.

2 Timothy 1:6,7
I remind you to fan into flame the gift of God, which is in you...
For God did not give us a spirit of timidity, but a spirit of power,
of love and of self-discipline.

CREATIVE CORRECTION

This book of the Bible is Paul's letter of instruction to another co-worker named Titus who was sent to Crete. Titus is encouraged to **reject what is corrupt, while embracing what is good** in these people. The Christian way of living was counter-cultural to the Cretans and would not be easily accepted and put into practice. **Titus is to accomplish this through the Holy Spirit empowered within him,** leading by example, and declaring God's grace to the world.

....

After finishing preschool, Blake went on to Kinder-Prep. While he was old enough and mature enough to enter Kindergarten, he struggled in two formative areas. The first of these areas was his fine motor skills. Even as a toddler, his writing instrument of choice was a mouse over a marker. He loved playing games and doing activities on the computer, but when it came to writing his name and coloring-in-the lines, he was clearly developmentally behind.

Through the grace of God, Blake was blessed with Mrs. Strote, a modern-day Titus teacher. In charge of a classroom full of four and five-year-olds not quite ready for Kindergarten surely qualified her for sainthood. She was proof that God gives the toughest battles to His most trusted soldiers. Mrs. Strote had the ability of seeing where each of her students uniquely struggled, while fully embracing where they each uniquely shined. With Blake, she noticed his weakness in writing straight away, but was also in awe of his intelligence. She told me that during free time many children in her class would play with every toy on the shelf and then say that they were bored. But Blake would use the same 30 minute timeframe and find many different ways to play with just one toy. Puzzles were his favorite, but when it came to coloring and drawing, he had zero interest.

Just a few weeks into the school year, Mrs. Strote asked me to help her come up with a way to motivate Blake in an activity that would exercise his fine motor muscles. Together we developed a plan. At home, Blake had a wooden puzzle of the United States that he had memorized and could accomplish with ease. I traced each piece of the puzzle onto a blank white piece of paper. I then gave him a box of crayons and told him that just for fun, I'd like him to choose one color for each state and that if two states were touching each other they could not be the same color. Blake was highly motivated and grabbed a red crayon and headed straight for California. He was a stickler for boundaries and was very careful not to get any of California's red color into Oregon or Nevada. He diligently and carefully colored for 15 minutes straight. Having never held a crayon for that long, I could tell his hand was getting tired. When I suggested he take a little break he took a deep breath and said, "Just South Dakota and then I'll stop."

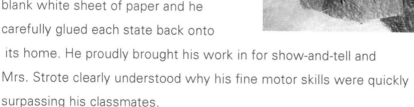

It took him about five days to finish his coloring project. The following week, I brought out the scissors and he now had to cut each state out individually. Again, he was very territorial and minded his borders with exact precision. I then traced the puzzle again on to a blank white sheet of paper and he carefully glued each state back onto its home. He proudly brought his work in for show-and-tell and Mrs. Strote clearly understood why his fine motor skills were quickly surpassing his classmates.

The other area of concern was in his speech. He wasn't very talkative, but when he did speak, it was quiet and quick. Often people would look

to me as his mother for interpretation after he spoke. Mrs. Strote was creative in developing this skill as well. She knew he was a good reader (No, I didn't tell her – she was blessed to find that out on her own). So one afternoon during storytime, she faked a sore throat and asked Blake if he could please help her finish reading the story to the class. What Blake lacked in speech, he made up for in obedience. He instantly stood up and went to the front of the classroom. Mrs. Strote handed him the book and took her place at the back of the classroom. After reading a few sentences, his wise teacher announced, "Blake, you are reading so well, but I'm getting older and my hearing isn't very good. Would you please read louder for me?" She truly was a *God-send* for him.

Before long, Blake had improved on expressing himself, but with increased communication, he then showed signs of a speech impediment. His language skills were still behind his peers. He struggled mostly with words that started with blended letters. For example the "TR" sound was pronounced with an "F" sound. So *train was fain, trace was face,* and when he told us he wanted his next birthday theme to be a truck party, his mispronunciations weren't quite as cute anymore.

Initially, his pediatrician was not too concerned and said he may just be speech delayed and would probably grow out of it, which put my mind at ease. But my dad, Blake's Papa, had been encouraging us since the truck party to take Blake to speech therapy. He was so insistent about getting Blake professional help that he even offered to pay for it -

which, if you know Big Al, you know he isn't one to seek outside help, especially if it costs money. So given his uncharacteristic passion to resolve this issue, and the fact that my dad was usually always right, I agreed and was surprisingly very impressed with the program. Each session was verbally challenging for Blake, but he always made great strides while he was there. He diligently practiced the flashcards he was given and with each visit, he would pretty much master the blend he was unable to pronounce the session before. His favorite homework assignment was to lick the lollipop they gave him each time he left. He was instructed to finish the whole thing without ever putting it inside his mouth. He needed to strengthen his tongue and this proved to be a great exercise.

By the time Blake started Kindergarten, there seemed to be nothing holding him back. In fact, I had mostly forgotten about his early struggles until his senior year of high school when he asked me to read over his Common Application for college admissions...

The Common Application

I sighed as I was asked by the doctor to attempt to read the flashcards yet again. Although my five-year-old self could not completely comprehend why I needed to go to speech class three times a week, I knew that something was not entirely right with me. Friends complained that they could not fully understand what I was trying to say, and teachers regularly asked me to slow down when I spoke. Although I was too young to grasp how important this life skill was, my struggles to efficiently communicate with my peers and elders had already begun to frustrate me.

Years later, I fidgeted as I stood in front of nearly 30 middle school students, all of whom were looking for a good reason to enroll in my high school. The admissions director at Crespi, who was also my soccer coach, had approached me weeks earlier and asked if I would be willing to volunteer my time towards pitching my school to perspective families. I knew that my speech issues were still very present, as speaking in front of any group, no matter the size, had terrified me throughout middle school and my first two years of high school. I had agreed to his request, not wanting to disappoint or let him down.

I knew I loved my school and wanted others to share in this school pride. I wanted to convey the impressive education and the family environment that Crespi offered to their students, but was not entirely convinced that I could illustrate this passion through words. At this point, I was past the point of return and had committed myself to representing my school the best I could. I felt chills run down my body as the director introduced me and left me alone in front of a crowd of complete strangers, with no choice but to overcome my fear of public speaking. Applause rang out from the audience as the last PowerPoint slide was completed and my presentation had run its course. I could tell by the excitement of the students that I had shown Crespi in a positive light and had peaked the interest of multiple potential scholars. I told myself throughout my speech that nobody would know if I made a mistake; wise advice that was given to me by the admissions director. Something clicked when I presented. I felt confident: something I had not

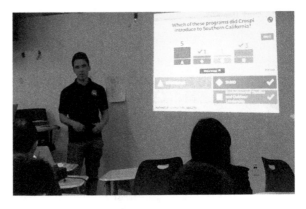

previously felt while public speaking. I also realized that I had successfully developed a former weakness into a strength that was acknowledged by the audience of peers and the administrators at my school.

I presented many times throughout the school year. I drove all over Southern California with the admissions director in pursuit of sharing the pride I had in my school with potential students. I was able to overcome my fears and insecurities and truly become more mature and transition from a scared child to a more confident, scholarly, and crucial member of my Crespi community. This entire experience helped me develop a critical life skill that will benefit me throughout my life, regardless of my profession.

Titus 2:6-8

Similarly, encourage the young men to be self-controlled. In everything set them an example by doing what is good. In your teaching show integrity, seriousness and soundness of speech that cannot be condemned.

BROWN PAPER PACKAGES

Paul finds himself in a difficult and delicate situation as he appeals to a man named Philemon. Paul explains to Philemon that he and Onesimus are to be **partners in sharing grace together through Jesus' healing mercy**. It is Paul's desire not to order Philemon to comply, but that he voluntarily **change his heart and live peacefully in a new situation.**

....

Shared Custody. A pair of words that when placed together, instantly make my heart drop an inch within my chest. On their own, these two words are quite positive. **Shared** means to lack selfishness and allow someone to enjoy something with you. **Custody** is to hold something within your care. Unfortunately, when these words are placed side by side, there is an understood broken family and a sense of dysfunction. Some divorced couples claim to have a healthy practice of this term. But for me, the concept is not natural or easy, and as much as my boys say, "We're fine," we all know it's not ideal.

While there is an official document that exists stating that I am responsible for my two sons 50 percent of the time, it doesn't keep me from being their mom 100 percent of the time. In the three years that our family has been split apart, this concept has been easy to know, but harder to show. How do I respect their dad's time and space with them, but still be there for them daily as their mom? It's taken some self-discipline for me to show them love when it's not "my day."

Last week, I was asking a friend if she thought I was enabling my boys by still making their lunches in high school. I confessed that I enjoy it so much that I text them on the weeknights they're at their dad's to ask if I can leave a lunch in my mailbox for each of them. It's my way of sweetening the deal, implying that they don't even need to come inside.

Proof that I won't hold their lunches hostage for a hug and a quick visit. It's an easy "YES" as they practically pass by my house anyway to get to school. I know their dad usually just has them buy lunch from the cafeteria, but this just makes me happy.

My friend's eyes filled with tears, and she helped me to see the beauty in what I was really doing: creating a way to peacefully connect with my boys - even on days when I've been told I'm not supposed to. Somewhere along the way, I had a change of heart about making sack lunches. When the boys were younger, I dreaded fitting that task into our hectic morning routine. But I suppose knowing that my senior and sophomore are on the cusp of no longer "brown bagging it," it has caused me to savor this opportunity. I've learned to embrace this chance to pray over them as I lovingly pack food that will soon be entering the very bodies I long to hold like I used to. I wonder if everyday around noon, as they open what has probably become more of a paper ball than a paper bag and begin pulling out distorted-shaped food contents, if they know how much they are loved. Do they know I get up extra early in order to have their brown paper packages ready for pick up should they need to head to school early?

Do they notice that I've packed each edible item specifically with them in mind? No mustard for Ryan, Fiber One bars for Blake? Are they aware that as they drive across the San Fernando Valley, I'm listening for their car? My mom's bedroom window looks out on to the front street so as I stand over her bed, exercising her legs like my dad used to do, I hope to catch a glimpse of them between the freshly opened curtains.

I always know when they are running late, because Blake slows down to about 5 mph, while Ryan leans way out of the passenger-side window to grab the goods.

In many ways, divorce eased me into kids growing up and leaving home completely. No parent has ever succeeded at keeping their kids little, regardless of how "functional" their family was. So we love them however we can, even if it seems enabling or slightly pathetic. And when the days come that I can't easily hold them close, I am grateful that I can call upon the One who can. I am blessed to have to share my time with my sons, as it reminds me how much I love them and deeply rely on the Lord for His provision; especially in my absence.

Philemon 1:6
I pray that your partnership with us in the faith may be effective in deepening your understanding of every good thing we share for the sake of Christ.

MY TERRIFIC MOM

The author and audience of Hebrews may be unclear, but its message is not: **Remain faithful to Jesus despite hardships and persecution.** The Book of Hebrews commends the faith of those who persevered in the Old Testament; inspiring us to continue on in such faith – knowing God has never and will never abandon His people.

....

There are a few things in this life we can truly count on: The sun rising and setting, incentive clothes never actually leaving your closet, and the answer you will get when you ask my mom, "How are you?" While the rest of the world is "fine," my mom's response is always "I'm terrific everyday of my life." Truthfully, this is what she says, no exaggeration - every time. Ask anyone who knows her, and they will tell you the same. For as far back as I can remember this has been her mantra, in good times and in bad.

When I was a senior in high school, I remember Mom dropping me off to join my friends to watch a varsity basketball game. Just as we drove onto campus, she announced to me, "I have M.S." *My whole body froze, but my mind went into high-speed. What? Multiple Sclerosis? Isn't that debilitating and even life threatening? What does that mean for our family? I can't even process that! How am I supposed to get out of this car now?* My whole world had just been turned upside-down!

For years, I questioned her timing in telling me. I was already halfway out the car door, anticipating a fun Friday night, only to spend it completely disconnected, shocked, and confused. But now, as a mother who's raised children myself, I get it. She probably tried to tell me the whole car ride there, maybe even for days or weeks before. She may have even made a promise to herself that she would finally say it before

I got out of the car that day. Whatever the case, I now know what it's like to share something difficult and life-altering with your child. So, while I'm at it, let me add one more thing to the list of things you can count on...there is no perfect way to tell your kids really hard things.

While M.S. is a deterioration of muscle over time, my mom is one of the strongest women I know. It's been 33 years since the day of that fateful drive when I reached some strong conclusions in my finite teenage mind. In that moment, I was convinced that my mom just told me she was dying, but in actuality she was about to show me how to live. Her faith did not waiver as she lived an appreciative life filled with hope.

A life that says, "Despite my circumstances I refuse to alter my attitude... I'm Karen Preston and I'm terrific everyday of my life, no one can take that from me." Over the years, I have witnessed this strength in different ways: Retiring from the airlines with unlimited free flights, but lacking the mobility to travel. Feeling the weight of others' eyes on

her as she took slow and steady steps down the aisle on both mine and my sister's wedding days. Wanting to participate more as a wife, mother, and grandmother, but physically limited by fatigue and accessibility.

In the last three decades I have watched my mom's eyes show brief moments of disappointment, followed by a lingering smile that genuinely states, "I am terrific everyday of my life!"

The truth is, things didn't pan out like my young self thought they would. Seeing as she didn't do much traveling, my mom was always available. Whether it be cutting and sorting teaching projects for me at the dining room table, watching my kids at a moments notice, or just having the time to sit and listen to my life - Mom's been there. I also got to watch my parents' relationship strengthen as they lived out what it means to love "in sickness and in health." The shock of Dad leaving this world before Mom was a reality that no one (especially my mom) could ever fathom. He was our strong rock! We all honestly believed he would out-live all of us. How shockingly scary this must have been for my mom. The one person that was always there to keep her safe, wasn't going to be there anymore. But again, Mom did not lose faith. It wasn't easy for me to watch her wheel up to Dad's hospice bed in the corner of our living room, but watching what she did when she got there inspired me. For the first time in a long time, they were at the same level. Both confined to contraptions that brought them eye-to-eye; my mom in her wheelchair and my dad in a bed with wheels. Seeing both of my parents in this state was difficult to look at but soon became one of the most beautiful pictures of love I have ever seen. Mom would gently slide Dad's hand into hers and talk about memories from the 55+ years they had been together. My dad was always so busy running around caring for my mom, and the house, and the shopping, and the garden. Any free time he had was spent either at the gym or creating masterpieces in his woodshop. He rarely sat and reminisced about precious moments of the past. Mom knew she didn't have much time left with him this side of Eternity, so she utilized every moment of the seven days it took for his body to shut down.

Although non-responsive, the doctors informed us that the ability to hear was still very much there. Listening in on my mom's still small voice recollect things like the day they first met, or the day they eloped in Lake Tahoe, or the day

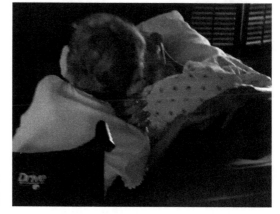

they brought me home from the hospital…it was beautiful. I remember praying a silent prayer as I watched the two of them together, "Lord, please bring me a love like that." In fact, during that time, I remember one night whispering in my dad's ear, "Dad, I promise you, I won't marry again unless I find someone who will love me like you loved Mom. Little did I know that those would be the last earthly words he would hear me say. The next morning, I woke to find him no longer with us.

Since then, I have stepped in as my mom's full-time caregiver. To my surprise, it's been just as much of a blessing for me as it has been for her. If you'd like to take a peek at what our life together entails, visit my website kimberlypreston.com to view our YouTube channel, MS at 80.

I love that my mom came into this world on January 12th and that my little Jeremiah came into this world on January 13th. These two people have both been emotionally and (at one point) physically connected to me. They have changed my world and inspired me to look outside of my circumstances and choose to faithfully be "terrific everyday of my life!"

Hebrews 11:1,2
Now faith is confidence in what we hope for and assurance about what we do not see. This is what the ancients were commended for.

RACHEL'S FAITH

The Book of James encourages us to see our hardships through a new lens. We are to view them as gifts that produce endurance. **God gives wisdom to all who ask for it in faith, without doubting that He is good regardless of our circumstances**. Genuine faith will always result in obedience to Jesus' teachings. Which means don't just listen to the Lord's words, but actually do what they say.

....

While I was still early on in my pregnancy with Jeremiah, a fellow teacher friend of mine posted on Facebook that she was in need of prayer during her pregnancy. In a nutshell this was her story: She had just gone in for her 20-week ultrasound and learned that her baby hadn't developed kidneys. There was also no vein going from the heart to where the kidneys should be that would carry essential fluids. Without these fluids, there would be no lung development. Her doctor said there was a very high probability that she could go full term, and when the baby is born he would be unable to breathe. Death would be imminent.

After sharing this news with my husband, we both agreed that we would have no idea what we would do in this situation. In addition to praying for God to perform a miracle for Rachel and her family, we selfishly prayed that God would not allow us to have to make such a decision with our own pregnancy. We both questioned if our faith was strong enough to continue to carry a baby that was destined to die at birth. I am not proud for feeling this way, but I didn't think I'd be able to. I have now grown to understand that when you are walking closely with God, He will equip you with everything good for doing His will. **(Hebrews 13:21)** And better yet, He will remind you our momentary troubles are achieving for us an eternal glory that far outweighs them all. **(2 Corinthians 4:17).**

Two weeks later, Rachel posted an update that the baby's condition had only further been confirmed by specialists and despite recommendations to take the baby now (abort), they would not. Here are her words, "Whether our baby stays alive for minutes or hours, we will treat it like a gift from the Lord for the opportunity to hold and love our little one, even if for a moment. If born not breathing, we will still thank our Lord for welcoming another of our children into His presence and for rescuing him from this world." Not only was Rachel living out her faith, but she continued to live it out everyday for the next four months as she did indeed carry this baby to full term. On March 8, 2012, her Facebook post read: Micah Aaron was born to this world at 3:37 a.m. weighing in at 3lbs. 12oz. He entered into eternal glory at 4:59 a.m. TO GOD BE THE GLORY.

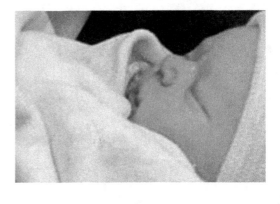

As I read her post, it had been seven weeks since my own loss. It was strange to think that inevitably, my baby Jeremiah would leave this world before hers even entered it. Our journeys were very different, but sadly, our outcomes were the same. I thought about how God had allowed our baby to be taken so quickly, yet equipped me immediately in that moment for all that He was about to do. I thought about how God allowed Rachel to continue to carry her baby long after his fatal diagnosis, during which time her family, friends, and even strangers were impacted and praying for a miracle that God knew He would not be granting. But in that same moment, He helped me realize, despite our heart-breaking disappointments, the miracle had already happened thousands of years ago. I wasted no time in posting to Rachel's wall what God had just posted on my heart: **From your arms into Jesus'**...

Praise God for making a way that we will all hold our babies again.
These words weren't just meant to offer my friend some comfort.
These words were to remind her of a truth that she had already been
living out everyday for the last 20 weeks. A truth that she knew with
such certainty, that it didn't matter what doctors or spectators thought
of her decision to carry. Rachel knew that God's timing would prove to
be better than anyone else's (Ecclesiastes 3:1,2). And by trusting in His
timing, He would give her a refuge that no other person could provide
her with (Psalm 62:8).

As I reflect back on the first time I got to know Rachel, years before
our two pregnancies, I am humbled. It was her turn to lead a devotional
during our morning teachers' meeting. She shared that she and her
husband were impacted greatly by their pastor's sermon: Praying for
God to Give Us Trials. As I re-read this passage (below) that she shared
with us that day, I get chills. I am once again in awe of our God, who
knows what lies ahead for each of His children. There is no situation in
your life that God has not already planned for. He will faithfully remind
you in the darkness what He has shown you in the light.

James 1:2-4

Consider it pure joy my brothers and sisters, whenever you face
trials of many kinds, because you know that the testing of your faith
produces perseverance. Let perseverance finish its work so that you
may be mature and complete, not lacking anything.

NEW HOPE

Jesus' disciple, Simon, was renamed Peter (a.k.a. "the rock") by Jesus and proves to be a leader that fellow Christians can lean on. Peter writes letters of encouragement to Christians facing hostility and harassment from neighboring Greeks and Romans. He offers guidance with practical instruction. He affirms them as **a family with a new identity** as God's children. He tells of a new hope they share and bear witness to in the love that Jesus brings. Peter teaches us that **life's hardships actually deepen our faith and restore us to greater strength** as we shift our focus on what is yet to come.

While hiking on a trail near my home, I stumbled upon this wild stalk that had suffered a pretty severe blow. Perhaps it weathered a difficult storm or someone along its path inflicted great harm upon it. But regardless of the circum-stances that caused such a life-changing shock, this stalk refused to give up hope. From a point of defeat, it somehow lifted its head toward Heaven and fought to stay alive. I'm not sure how much time had to pass before it became healthy and strong enough to produce new blossoms. I'm sure it needed to find nourishment within its foundation and receive daily light from the sun. But if you look closely, you will see buds of new life ready to open. Clearly the other stalks on the hillside were untouched by such a hardship and were already in full bloom. While those stalks appear to be much stronger, I would have to disagree.

Strength isn't defined by how tall or full of blossoms you are, it's defined by how willing you are to get up after being knocked down.

To accept such life-altering circumstances and forge ahead despite no longer knowing what your next season of life may look like, takes a great deal of strength.

Strength is having the ability to trust God to make a way, even when it seems impossible. Like this stalk, I too had suffered a severe blow when my marriage of nearly two decades ended. It wasn't just the relationship that was severed, it was the loss of hopes to come: family BBQs, family game nights, family vacations, (pretty much any term you can grammatically put the word family in front of). I didn't understand that we could still be a family with one man down. Years after my divorce, I was in a healthier state of mind and I could now focus on a hopeful future, despite circumstantial attempts to break me.

At the top of my "new hope wish-list," I wanted yearly family vacations with my boys. I knew the odds were stacked against me as they were already both in college and I had taken on the responsibility as my mom's full time caregiver - indefinitely. Getting them to willingly commit to going away with just me for a few days out of the year would take some creativity, bathed in divine intervention. I gained hope by thinking back on successful uses of these combined qualities in the past, like the Mother's Day they completely forgot about me.

It was the first Mother's Day in 15 years that I walked into the kitchen wondering where my standard box of Entenmann's chocolate donuts, flowers, and card could possibly be. My two teenagers woke up at noon and treated the day as any other - that is until they checked their social media. Based off their apologies as they clamored down the stairs, I'm guessing they were reminded after reading posts of well wishes and shout-outs to other mothers. "Anything you want Mom, we are so sorry," came their mid-day plea.

Creativity and divine intervention – activate! (Unless you grew up watching the Wonder Twins on "The All-New Super Friends Hour" in the '70's and '80's, you won't truly appreciate that.) Anyway, that was the year I received the best Mother's Day gift I've ever gotten in my whole life. I told my boys that all I wanted was a hug, like the heartfelt one they just gave me – but I want it every morning for a whole year. In the moment, they quickly agreed and thought they got out of that pickle quite easily. But after a week they needed some reminding, which I consistently gave them. And after about a month it became a habit, and then after a full year, they forgot to stop. To this day, my boys both hug me with ease. It was not a good Mother's Day, but what came from it was better than all my other Mother's Days put together. That's living-hope in action: hurtful, damaging and disappointing in the moment, only to rise up and conquer at the end.

Recalling this event and feeling armored up, I spent the next few weeks applying equal parts prayer and research to my new hope of family travel. I had accrued points through our timeshare to stay in a few pre-selected destinations. I contacted each of my boys in September and told them, "This Christmas, instead of giving you cash to use on who knows what, my gift to you is taking you on a trip. Your gift to me is going. Here are your choices: Palm Springs, San Diego, or San Francisco." They both independently chose San Francisco without hesitation. We went and had a fabulous four days

away, just us. They got to go someplace they'd never been and never had to think about a gift for me, for I (yet again) had gotten the very gift I wanted. Their presence was my present.

Update

Despite 2020 being the year of unpredictability, especially in the area
of travel, I booked our second annual mother-sons adventure for mid
December in Lake Tahoe. Due to Covid-19, I hadn't seen Blake since the
year before on our first mother-sons trip. I was hopeful that the three of
us could social distance in the crisp mountain air together. We safely
enjoyed five beautiful days of hiking, snowboarding, playing family
games, and cooking family dinners. Two days after our trip, Lake Tahoe
shut down to visitors due to social distancing orders. I am so grateful
that by God's grace we were protected and able to continue our
new-hope family tradition.

A BOY AND HIS PAPA

Many of the key ideas in these three short books are a continuation from Jesus' teachings in the Gospel of John. The chapter of John in my book entitled "Made Known" just so happens to also pave the way into this chapter's story as well (Unplanned by me, but I'm sure planned by God). First, Second, and Third John share the themes of **life, truth, and love, reminding God's people that their actions speak even louder than their words.**

....

Now that my 19-year-old has been away at college for two months, I decided to organize his old room a bit. I warned him before he left that I would be tackling this project, so I didn't anticipate coming across anything of great interest. I mostly found myself sifting through stacks of old papers and notebooks from his high school days, saved because of the time invested in them, but really never to be looked at again. Today I stumbled upon a manila envelope filled with letters of love and encouragement to him. Just one year ago, I played a part in collecting these letters for his Senior High School Retreat. Until this moment, I had not realized how many people had actually followed through with my request and sent letters into the school. These letters were delivered to him during the retreat and then brought back home to be cherished. Today I fought back the temptation to carefully open and read them ALL! Instead, I marveled at the thickness and weight of the packed envelope and decided to take solace in knowing my boy is loved and cherished by so many.

As I worked my way over to his nightstand, I opened the top drawer to find one letter separated from the others. I wondered why he might want to keep this one closer and more easily accessible. The temptation was just too great, so this one I did unfold. I knew immediately from the unique cursive lettering it was from my dad, Blake's papa. Tears welled up in my eyes as I recognized his handwriting and a flood of emotions surfaced. I thought about how my mom had shared with me, that after years of allowing my dad to sign his name to her cards and letters, for the first time she insisted, "You need to write your own." So, I guess he did. And - as if further proof were needed- it is written on an upside-down piece of notebook paper. That is so my dad.

If you are his sibling, wife, daughter, grandchild, or treasured friend the penmanship may be familiar, and prick your heart as it did mine. For all others, I've written out his letter and attached it here as well:

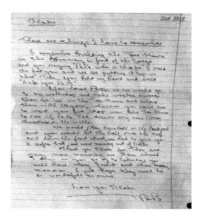

Blake

These are things I love to remember

I remember building the tree house in the driveway in front of the garage and you saying, "Papa who is this for." I said that it's for you and we are putting it up in that Tree. You held my hand and said, "Ank you Papa".

You loved pirates so we would go to my workshop and make wooden swords and then go up in the tree house and color them with crayons. Whenever you came over to visit your first stop was the tree house to see if Papa had drawn any new Disney characters on the walls.

We would play baseball in the backyard and you would hit the ball over the roof and down the front street. We had to give you a softer bat; we were running out of balls.

Thank you Blake for these and many more memories we have shared. I know as you go off to College you will have many friends and share many memories...I just hope they will be as wonderful as mine.

Love you Blake
Papa

Three months after writing this special note to his grandson, my dad passed away. I imagine this letter found its way to the nightstand somewhere around that time. Blake was my dad's very first grandchild and was the one who deemed

him "Papa," for all future grandchildren to follow suit. To our family, the name Papa came to mean "Love in action."

Oh how I enjoyed watching my strong, wise, and set-in-his-ways father live up to this given name. He matched my son's child-like excitement during every moment they spent together. While I wish our time with him had been longer, I'm so grateful to know that he left this world

with such treasured memories in the forefront of his mind, and that those memories were imprinted and set apart as something special to a boy who grew up to become an amazing adult, as a result of his Papa's love.

YOU BROUGHT JESUS TO A BAR?

This book of the Bible was written by a servant of Jesus Christ named Jude. He writes these words to **those who have been called by God the Father and will encounter godless men**, who change the grace of our God into a license for immorality. The entire book is only one chapter long, but serves as an excellent reminder to believers that their faith is being demonstrated in how they live and interact with others, especially **those who deny Jesus Christ, our only Sovereign and Lord.**

....

There is a famous line from the movie "Sweet Home Alabama," where Reese Witherspoon's character travels back home and runs into a friend from high school. "Look at you! You have a baby…in a bar," she says. When this movie came out, I was married and raising two little boys. Just the thought of going to a bar, let alone with a baby, was hysterically funny to me. Later I remember hearing a sermon at church where my pastor explicitly said that Christians should never go to bars, that there is nothing but temptation and toxins to be found there. Clearly, the idea of bringing something as pure as a baby or a believer into such an establishment is an understood no-no.

Well, about a year after my divorce, my outgoing, confident friend Jessica felt compelled to nudge me into socializing with other singles. She thought perhaps happy hour would be a place to comfortably ease me back into talking with men after more than 20 years of being loyal to just one. I was a bit hesitant, but felt that being in a room full of people that showed up to relax and socialize might be a nice change from my Friday night movie on the couch. I knew my pastor might not agree with this decision, but God calls us to go out into the world … just be sure to not leave Him at home when you do. So out we went.

It was actually rather empowering, stepping out of my comfort zone and entering an unfamiliar place with a solid sense of self and an intuitive wisdom that comes with life experience and maturity. Most of the time, Jessica and I just sat and talked and had minimal interaction with the people around us. She too had been divorced before and was now happily remarried. She'd walked in my shoes and was now on the other side and able to understand that this stage in my life would be a time of pruning that would lead to growth.

At one point, a tall, handsome, fair-haired, blue-eyed man approached our table and struck up a conversation with us. "So how do you two know each other?" he asked.

> Without hesitation, Jessica responded, "From church. And we host a mid-week Bible study together. Would you like to come?" (I told you she was outgoing and confident.)

> "Really?! I find the Bible pretty hypocritical. I mean saying Jesus is the only way to Heaven is pretty harsh. Do you guys actually believe that?" he retorted.

I was usually rather reserved when it came to talking to men I knew nothing about, but this guy sparked something inside me. I suddenly found the desire to be bold, to put myself out there, and get personal with a guy on a barstool.

> "Yes. We do believe that," I replied. Jessica gave me a wink, as if to say, "you got this."

> His eyes opened widely and his eyebrows shot up. "So you're saying that you get to go to Heaven and I don't?"

> "No, I'm saying, I get to go to Heaven ... but I really have no idea where you're going. You see it's not my place to judge you." I said calmly. "The Bible states that God gives that job to Jesus, and even

then – His judgment isn't given until the end of one's life (John 5:22). Thankfully, His mercies are new every morning – and I have no idea how merciful the Lord will be to you (Lamentations 3:23)." I could tell Jessica was proud of my boldness, but truthfully it was her bold introduction and fellow Christian presence that gave me such confidence.

After a contemplative pause he said, "Huh, I've never heard it put that way before."

"The truth is, your fate isn't based on my belief, only my fate is. God looks at the heart and He knows yours, I don't," came the words that didn't feel like my own - and I hadn't even gotten my drink yet.

The rest of the evening Mr. Tall Blond hung out with the three of us: me, Jessica, and Jesus. Our conversations were light and comical. I enjoyed my one adult beverage and even joined him on the dance floor before saying goodbye. As Jessica and I turned to leave, he said, "I didn't realize Christians could be as cool as the two of you. Thank you for showing me a different side. Take care."

In the very short book of Jude we are encouraged to be merciful to those who doubt; snatch others from the fire and save them; to others show mercy mixed with fear – hating even the clothing stained by corrupted flesh (Jude 1:22-23). To me this means meet people where they're at! True, there are patrons that frequent bars with stained clothing and corrupted flesh that we should mix our mercy with fear and hate the suit they choose to wear. There may be others who are literally headed straight into the fire and the urgent response is to snatch them up and save them before they die. And then there are those like the guy I encountered at the bar: doubting, but willing to question. To those we are to simply be merciful. We don't need to tackle the whole Bible in one night. Just focus on the issue that the doubter has. This man's issue was that Christianity is harsh and judgmental. By the end of the night he may not have known Jesus as his personal Lord and Savior, but at least he didn't leave the bar with the same misconception he came in with.

Sometimes we plant, sometimes we water, and sometimes we reap. That night, as we planted ourselves at the high top table for four, we were given the chance to also plant a biblical truth in another's heart. I pray at some point others will come water this seed, and eventually this man will reap the reward of knowing Jesus personally and one day have a life with Him in Eternity. It rarely happens all at once, and as Christians we are encouraged to remember that with God there are no such things as small successes, for He will do great things with them.

Funny, like many chance encounters during happy hour, I don't even remember the guy's name. But I will never forget the night we stayed true to our identity and friendly and confidently brought Jesus to a bar.

Jude vs. 17-21

But dear friends, remember what the apostles of our Lord Jesus Christ foretold. They said to you, "In the last times there will be scoffers who will follow their ungodly desires. These are the men who divide you, who follow mere natural instincts and do not have the Spirit. But you dear friends...keep yourself in God's love as you wait for the mercy of our Lord Jesus Christ to bring you to eternal life.

LIFE ASSURANCE

Jesus gives John a revelation of what will one day take place at the
end of time when the world will face eternal judgment. Amidst the
beasts with horns and many eyes, an evil trinity, the Lake of Fire, and
other obscure coded messages – there is a lamb. To me, a lamb is the
most peaceful, gentle symbol that could possibly exist. **As believers
in Christ, our names are sealed and can never be blotted out of the
Book of Life**. We have been set apart and will be rescued from the parts
of Revelation that speak of devastation and a fate that is unfathomable.

....

"Mommy, is your name written in the Lamb's Book of Life?"
questioned my five-year-old upon bursting through the front door.
I hadn't even heard the carpool drop him off, so he caught me
completely by surprise.

"Hi Blake, how was your day?" I asked while attempting to
re-center.

"Today my teacher told us about the Lamb's Book of Life, and
I need to know if your name is in it," he said insistently.

At this point in my spiritual walk, I had never made it past Chapter Two
in Revelation. I remember in my high school youth group one of the
leaders told us that as Christians we would already be in Heaven during
the years that followed the Rapture, so I took that as an excuse to stop
reading. I figured I was covered and reading about what non-believers
would be left to face would only upset me. But I did not anticipate this
line of questioning from my kid in Pre-K when I would one day become
a mom. So I now regretted that I hadn't read on.

Still a bit confused I asked, "I don't know, is your name in it?"

Without hesitation he responded, "Yes! Because I believe for sure that Jesus is God's son and that He died for our sins and that He rose back to life after the cross. Unless you believe that, your name can't be in the book."

"Well, then my name is for sure in the book," I told him.

"Okay good, then you'll get to go to Heaven," he said with a sigh of relief. "... now I just need to talk to Dad about this."

Needless to say, that night I spent some time in the Book of Revelation. Sure enough, the Book of Life is mentioned numerous times throughout. Nothing impure will ever enter it (Heaven), nor will anyone who does what is shameful or deceitful, but only those whose names are written in the Lamb's Book of Life; (Revelation 21:27) is the reference that I most comfortably settled upon.

At first, Blake's urgency was a little jarring, as it forced one to view faith as a quick yes or no answer. I highly doubt his teacher used this scare tactic when discussing the Lamb's Book of Life with her Kinder-Prep students that day in class. I know full well that my son views things very literally. A few weeks before this experience, he had come home telling me all about a woman at school named "Miss Conduct" who kicks (insert literal kicking motion) kids out of school if they are bad.

After inquiring the following day with his teacher, I got a bit more clarity on this: The teacher was reviewing the school rules with the class and told them that repeated disobedience would result in a "misconduct". One of his classmates blurted out, "that means getting kicked out of school." The teacher agreed that if a student continued their poor behavior, getting kicked out would be a possibility. Blake had the wording right, he just took it a bit too literally. Anyway, I figured my extremely impressionable child walked away with some very concrete thinking in this case too.

Many years later, January 2020 to be exact, I would study the Book of Revelation at the Community Bible Study I was attending. This time, I didn't shy away from reading the uncomfortable parts, for I knew God's character. **I didn't mind seeing Him as a Lion for I already knew Him as a Lamb**. Throughout the study, I reflected back on that moment with Blake 18 years prior. He wasn't being overdramatic, his reaction and urgency were, in my opinion now, right on. He wasn't worried about his own fate. In his pure, child-like faith, he somehow understood his place in Heaven was sealed. His immediate concern was for the ones he loved.

As my study in Revelation continued, I was surprised to find so many parallels between my own life experiences and the concepts in Revelation that I had once struggled with. Revelation 16:15 speaks of the end times coming unexpectedly like a thief in the night. It goes on to say, Blessed is the one who stays awake and remains clothed, so as not to go naked and be shamefully exposed. I love the poetic symbolism of staying alert and constantly clothing myself in attributes and values that show evidence of the condition of my heart. A visual of this truth that I hold dear, comes from Ryan at age seven. As I leaned over his bed one evening to kiss him goodnight, I realized that he was fully dressed, shoes and all. When I questioned why he was wearing his clothes to bed he told me, "In case I get kidnapped in the middle of the night, this is the outfit I want to be wearing." The innocence of his heart serves as a beautiful reminder that when Jesus does return, I want to be clothed in righteousness, wearing my spiritual best and having my feet readied to walk wherever He leads.

Revelation 14:1 is also a verse that I'm able to assign another visual from my life to. It speaks of the Lamb standing before those who had His name and His Father's name written on their foreheads. In one of my earlier chapters, I shared about the precious children of Uganda who were so excited to accept my simple gift of a sticker. Not just some of the children, but all of the children, everywhere I went, wanted me to place the sticker in the center of their forehead. Even when I tried to hand a child a sticker, they would rarely take it, and instead they would point to the exact spot on their forehead they wanted me to place it.

When I asked my friend Abby why this was, she told me that the children want <u>you</u> to stick it, for it meant receiving a blessing from a Mzungu. They desired to have it on their foreheads so that everyone can see and know that they are blessed and loved.

May my testimony of faith in God's Book be evident for all to see in this book. Oh what a blessing it has been to let Him write His story on my heart.

Revelation 22:7

Behold, I am coming soon! Blessed is he who keeps the words of the prophecy in this book.

NOW THAT YOU'VE READ MY JOURNEY THROUGH THE BOOKS
OF THE BIBLE, HOW WOULD YOU FEEL ABOUT SHARING YOURS?

It's Real to Me Too is a journal that accompanies *It's Real to Me*, and
is available for purchase. Just go to kimberlypreston.com and click on
the order link. This journal is creatively designed to give you the space
and guidance to make the Bible real to you too. It's such a beautiful
revelation to see your personal journey through the eyes of your Creator.

CPSIA information can be obtained
at www.ICGtesting.com
Printed in the USA
JSHW050940230721
17160JS00002B/7